EYFS: LANGUAGE OF LEARNING

A HANDBOOK TO PROVOKE, PROVIDE AND EVALUATE LANGUAGE DEVELOPMENT

BY ALEX BEDFORD
AND JULIE SHERRINGTON

Orders: please contact Hachette UK Distribution, Hely Hutchinson Centre, Milton Road, Didcot, Oxfordshire, OX11 7HH. Telephone: +44 (0)1235 827827. Email education@hachette.co.uk. Lines are open from 9 a.m. to 5 p.m., Monday to Friday.

ISBN: 9781398390058

First published in 2023 by
John Catt from Hodder Education,
An Hachette UK Company
15 Riduna Park, Station Road,
Melton, Woodbridge IP12 1QT
Telephone: +44 (0) 1394 389850

www.johncatt.com

A catalogue record for this title is available from the British Library

Acknowledgements

With immense thanks to Julie Sherrington for bravely joining me and navigating this adventure so skilfully. You bring brilliance and expertise.

To Darren Woodward, Lauren Meadows and Sherise Daly for your ever-present wisdom, endless belief and patience.

To the EYFS settings and schools who have supported, guided and worked with us:

Houldsworth Valley Primary Academy, Suffolk

Lisa Tweed, Sophie Baldwin, Katie Collings

Abbots Green Academy, Suffolk

Ang Morrison, Rod Marsh, Sophie Newson

Langer Primary Academy, Suffolk

Toni Kittle, Magda Metcalfe

Brambleside Primary School, Northamptonshire

Drew Brown, Natalie Goosey, Emma Lee, Kayleigh Beale

John Scurr Primary School, London

Maria Lewington, Keeley Alborough, Evelyn McSweeney, Ruby Goodchild, Lily Pettitt, Lotus Suffell, Sophie Lewis, Joanne Power

St Mary's Catholic Primary School (NPCAT), Middlesbrough

Anna McClurey, Jenny Hurley, Joe Stammers, Jack Carey, Mary Brown

Whitefield Primary School, Liverpool

Jill Wright, Marie Beale, Emma Doran

This book is also dedicated to all the folk who have ever worked in, taught and taken inspiration from early years practice, including the inspirational Mrs B and her Reception class!

Kind words

What does it actually mean for an early years setting to be language-rich? What does it really mean to make the kind of progress in spoken communication that lays firm foundations for later learning? The fascinating response to these questions in this book describes progress in terms of language functions – it's not just about developing syntax and broadening vocabulary, but doing so in order to communicate across different language functions. Some kinds of talk enable children to describe and elaborate, others to reason logically and yet others to empathise or imagine. The lucky practitioners who get their hands on a copy of this book will find themselves guided through a hugely useful and very practical tool for planning language-rich experiences.

Clare Sealy, head of education improvement, Guernsey

This book will be the go-to resource for practitioners who want a clear, user-friendly way to develop children's language in the EYFS setting. Inspired by Joan Tough's language development framework, it offers educators a way to understand, plan and sequence high-quality conversations to help develop shared thinking, communication and language. We love the clarity of the writing and the illustrations, and the worked examples bring the approach to life. We can't wait to go into schools that use this approach and see the children thrive!

John Walker and Tita Beaven, Sounds-Write

This is so helpful for colleagues. It provides an elegant structure on which to base our judgements about how well our pupils are getting on in the EYFS. And, just as importantly, it provides prompts to elevate and deepen our practice. A really smart resource – great work!

Mary Myatt, education adviser, writer and speaker

About the authors

With more than 29 years of experience in education as a teacher, headteacher and leading adviser for school improvement, **Alex Bedford** now supports Unity Schools Partnership and its Research School, working across the UK and abroad. Alex is the creator and author of the highly acclaimed *Pupil Book Study* series (originally published in 2021) and has worked as an associate consultant for the Institute of Education, UCL. His curriculum writing and resources have been highly praised by Professor Rob Coe and by Clare Sealy (head of education improvement, Guernsey).

You may be surprised to learn that Alex did not engage well at school and spent most of his secondary schooling in the 'remedial stream'. His parents were even told not to 'waste' tutoring money on him. Alex's career took an interesting journey through the Youth Training Scheme in an entomology lab and several years of employment in food technology labs, where he worked on the viscosity of jam in Jammie Dodgers and recipes for Marks & Spencer. Further education led Alex to eventually train as a primary school teacher. He has never looked back. His rule for school is simple: teach with excellence and never write anyone off. According to all the SEND experts Alex has worked with, he channels his ADHD superpower to his advantage, so he can be the most positive and productive person he can.

Husband to Becky (a phenomenal Reception teacher) and proud father of Jack and Finn, Alex is called to adventure and is regularly drawn to the sea and mountains.

With more than 22 years of experience in education as a teacher, headteacher, school improvement consultant and early reading expert, **Julie Sherrington** now leads early years for GLF Schools, a large trust with 35 primary schools and 20 nurseries. She also works for Greenfields Education as an early years lead and lead evaluator.

Julie is passionate about getting early education right to improve the life chances of every unique individual who enters our schools. She is often found reading and talking about the profound impact of communication, language and physical development on all other aspects of learning and life, and she has a healthy obsession with oracy.

Avoiding assumptions: things you need to know

I want you to know that Julie and I are not gurus who have it all sorted. We are humans who lead, teach and write about our experiences from the classroom. We work with incredible children, teachers and schools across the world.

Writing this book has been a journey of trying to make sense of the most impactful evidence that lies in a sea of misinformation, as well as a mission to draw on nearly 50 years of combined experience in education. We have tried to break down the things that we have learned as teachers and leaders.

The books we have chosen help practitioners to check that pupils are securing the foundational knowledge needed for key stage 1 as well as crucial language development.

EYFS: Language of Learning lives within the Pupil Book Study family. When I began researching and writing this book, I knew that, as effective as the Pupil Book Study framework was, it needed to be refined to meet the demands of the early years foundation stage (EYFS).

We acknowledge that early learning goals (ELGs) are end-of-year outcomes – they are not a curriculum. They exist to prompt thought and discussion about how well pupils are securing the knowledge they need for a good level of development and KS1 readiness.

Contents

Chapter 1

The purpose of this book

What is this book about?

1. **A language development framework** that enables early years practitioners to effectively lead high-quality, structured conversations that sustain shared thinking.

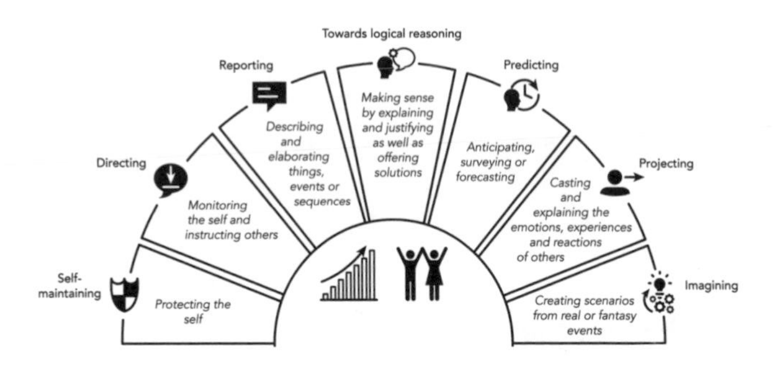

2. **An overview of essential research** that enhances early years practice.

3. **A refocus on physical development** to position and explain why this prime area of the EYFS impacts on child learning and development.

4. **Worked examples** of how to use the language development framework with beautiful books.

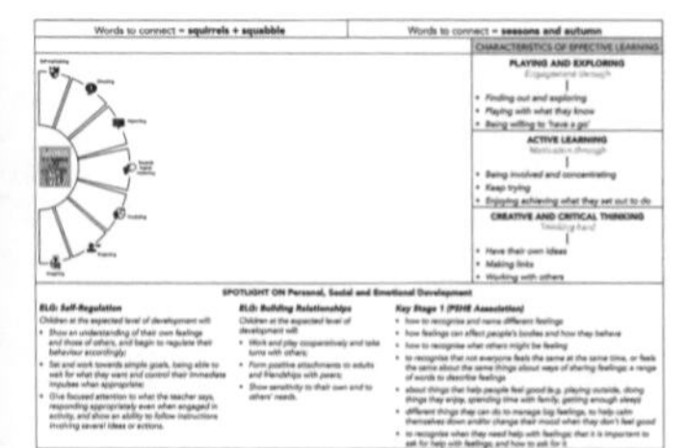

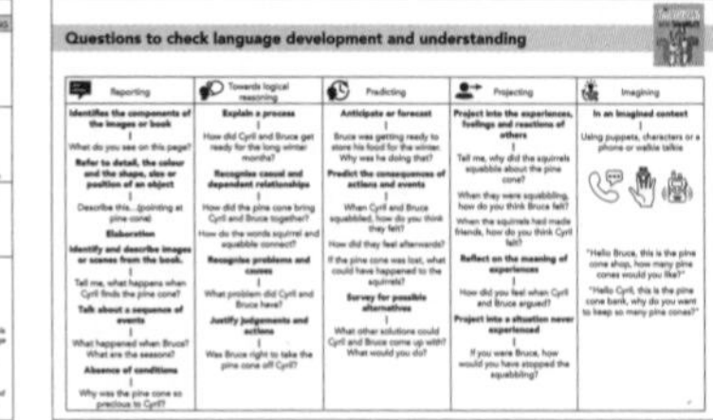

Our inspiration

Inspired by Joan Tough's research and publications from the 1970s, this handbook, *EYFS: Language of Learning*, interweaves the most current thinking around child development with our representation of Tough's language development framework.

The purpose of this book is to provide early years practitioners with an incredibly accessible and evidence-informed language framework that can be used at the point of provision and as an evaluation tool – just like the Pupil Book Study framework, but for the EYFS.

It's a true skill to respond to young children with precise and developmental questioning, statements or provocations. Investing in fully understanding this framework and being able to insightfully sustain shared thinking with young children will bring about a shared language of learning.

'Spoken words have so short an existence that they are gone before they can be fully examined'

Tough, 1973

Tough's language development framework is adaptable to the myriad learning opportunities and experiences present within an EYFS setting. Although it is a developmental toolkit, the framework is also responsive to the provision.

EYFS: Language of Learning asks the question: what do children need to experience more of in their EYFS settings? And how do you know?

What is this book?

It is...

1. **A handbook** for schools, teachers and practitioners to use as a source of professional development and current thinking.

2. **A provocation** to check the ambition of the school.

3. **A guide** to support teachers and practitioners to plan for and check the language development opportunities, provision and experiences they offer.

4. **A reference point** for amazing practice and clear explanations of important factors affecting the physical development of children.

5. **A questioning framework** with worked examples and templates to inspire teachers and practitioners to think hard about their interactions and the impact their words have on children.

It is...

1. **Not designed to teach children to read**. The book is a holistic language framework to be used intelligently in response to the areas of learning in which children need to become a little more expert.

2. **Not a long-winded narrative**. This book is designed with the practitioner in mind – lots of provocation and brilliant content for professional development.

3. **Not going to reduce creativity in the EYFS**. Quite the opposite – it enriches language and enables pupils to thrive in an environment that values each individual and their interests across the curriculum.

4. **Not restrictive**. The examples are a springboard for your professional development and growth. Take our work and build on it to enhance opportunities, provision and experiences for your pupils.

Where do language, stories, books and reading appear in the EYFS statutory framework?

Extracted from the Department for Education's *Statutory Framework for the Early Years Foundation Stage* (2023)

Communication and language: summary
'Reading frequently to children, and engaging them actively in stories, non-fiction, rhymes and poems, and then providing them with extensive opportunities to use and embed new words in a range of contexts, will give children the opportunity to thrive. Through conversation, story-telling and role play, where children share their ideas with support and modelling from their teacher, and sensitive questioning that invites them to elaborate, children become comfortable using a rich range of vocabulary and language structures.'

ELG: Speaking
'Offer explanations for why things might happen, making use of recently introduced vocabulary from stories, non-fiction, rhymes and poems when appropriate.'

ELG: Listening, attention, understanding
'Listen attentively and respond to what they hear with relevant questions, comments and actions when being read to and during whole class discussions and small group interactions.'

Literacy: summary
'It is crucial for children to develop a life-long love of reading. Reading consists of two dimensions: language comprehension and word reading. Language comprehension (necessary for both reading and writing) starts from birth. It only develops when adults talk with children about the world around them and the books (stories and non-fiction) they read with them, and enjoy rhymes, poems and songs together.'

ELG: Reading comprehension
- 'Demonstrate understanding of what has been read to them by retelling stories and narratives using their own words and recently introduced vocabulary.
- Anticipate – where appropriate – key events in stories.
- Use and understand recently introduced vocabulary during discussions about stories, non-fiction, rhymes and poems and during role-play.'

Communication and language
Personal, social and emotional development
Physical development
Conversation
Vocabulary
Story-telling
Stories
Positive sense of self
Attention
Language
Communication
Literacy
Mathematics
Understanding the world
Expressive arts and design

Understanding the world: summary
'Listening to a broad selection of stories, non-fiction, rhymes and poems will foster their understanding of our culturally, socially, technologically and ecologically diverse world. As well as building important knowledge, this extends their familiarity with words that support understanding across domains.'

About early learning goals
The ELGs should not be used as a curriculum or in any way to limit the wide variety of rich experiences that are crucial to child development, from being read to frequently to playing with friends.

ELG: Understanding the world – past and present
'Know some similarities and differences between things in the past and now, drawing on their experiences and what has been read in class. Understand the past through settings, characters and events encountered in books read in class and storytelling.'

ELG: Understanding the world – people, culture and communities
- 'Describe their immediate environment using knowledge from observation, discussion, stories, non-fiction texts and maps.
- Know some similarities and differences between different religious and cultural communities in this country, drawing on their experiences and what has been read in class.
- Explain some similarities and differences between life in this country and life in other countries, drawing on knowledge from stories, non-fiction texts and – when appropriate – maps.'

ELG: Being imaginative and expressive
'Invent, adapt and recount narratives and stories with peers and their teacher. Perform songs, rhymes, poems and stories with others, and – when appropriate – try to move in time with music.'

Golden threads running through this book

Communication and language

As we articulate the language development framework throughout this book, all the resources we have written permeate and develop the communication and language area of learning within the EYFS and beyond.

Personal, social and emotional development

The language development framework pays close attention to the way children regulate, communicate and attend. Using the framework to plan provision supports all areas of personal, social and emotional development (PSED).

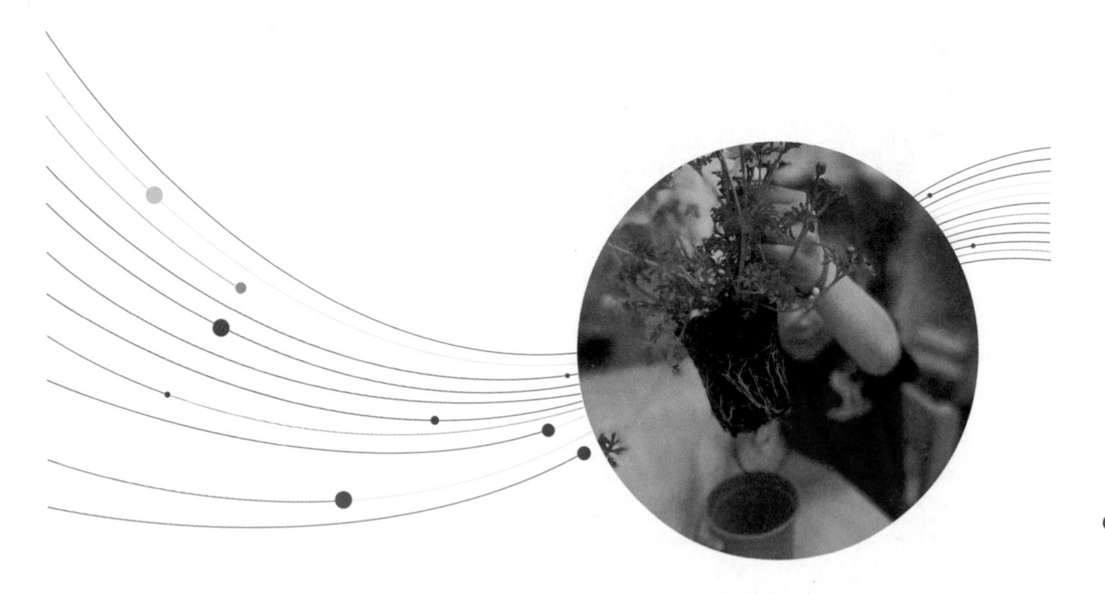

Physical development

We know more about the impact of physical development on cognition and learning than ever before. Chapter 4 explains more about the impact of immature sensory systems and why physical development is a prime area of learning.

Communication and language questions every setting should ask

Extracted from the Department for Education's *Statutory Framework for the Early Years Foundation Stage* (2023)

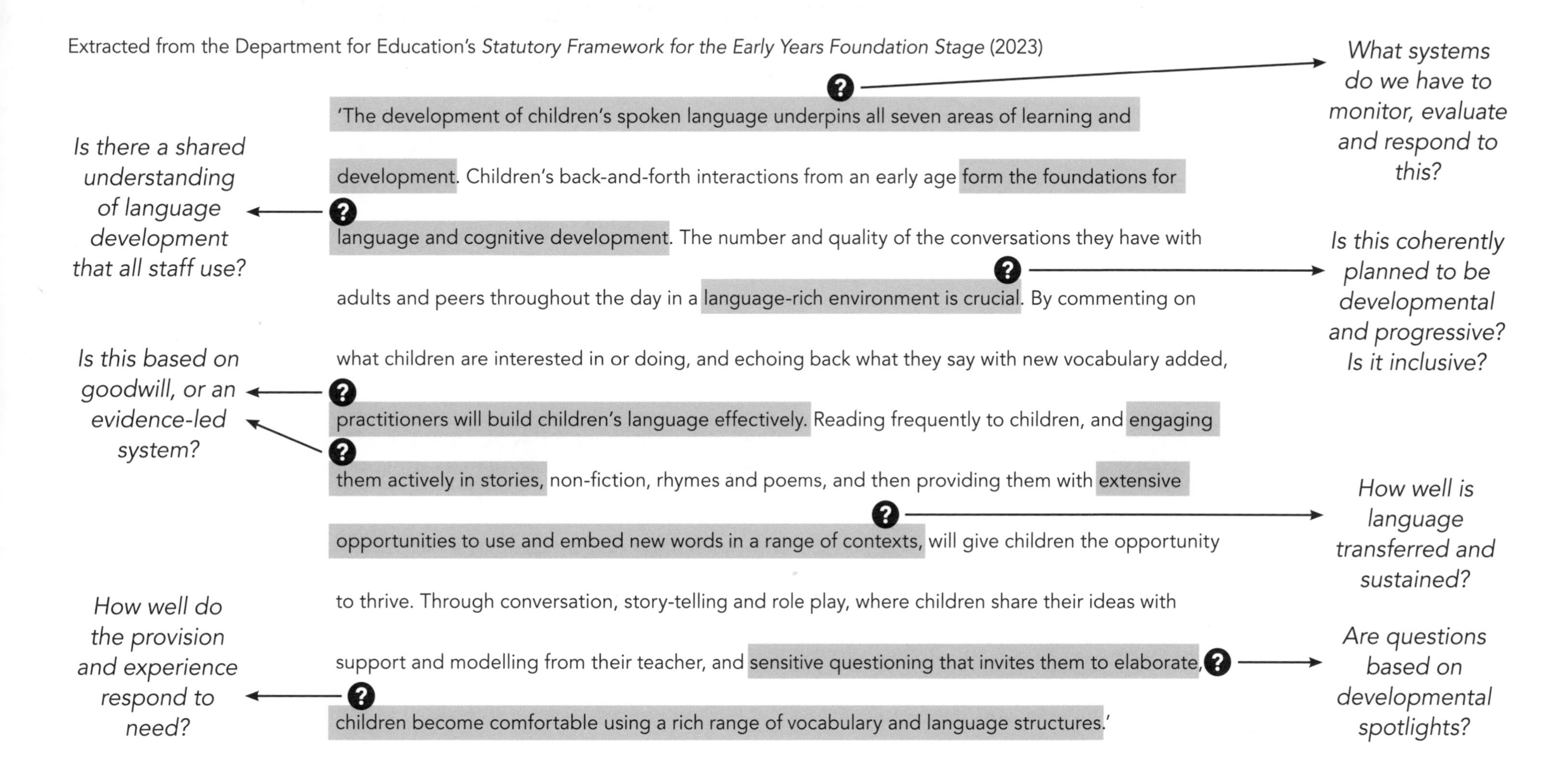

Ask yourself...

If you were asked these questions, how would you answer?

1. How ambitious is your setting in securing excellence in communication and language development?

2. Explain how communication and language are developed throughout your setting and the research that sits behind this. What does a language-rich environment actually mean?

3. How have you achieved consistency with all staff in supporting communication and language development across your setting?

4. What is your approach to staff training for communication and language development, and how much time is spent on this? For example, ShREC approach, EEF Evidence Store, direct vocabulary instruction.

5. How well do all staff know each and every child's communication and language needs, and how do you ensure that pupils who are behind their expected developmental mileposts catch up?

6. How do you know that the opportunities, provision and experiences in your enabling environment(s) are developing children's language effectively? What mechanisms are in place to check this? How do pupils have opportunities to retrieve and practise the language they know in different contexts?

Chapter 2

Introducing and reimagining Joan Tough's language development framework

A toolkit for language development: Joan Tough MA, PhD

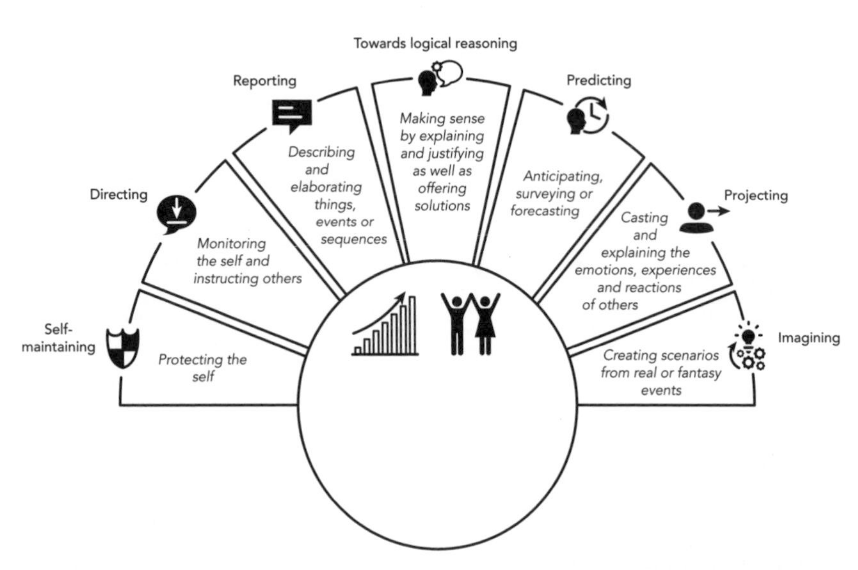

Taking inspiration, I redrew and reimagined Joan Tough's language development framework (1977a). I look back and wish I'd had Tough's framework to hand when I wrote my first book, *Pupil Book Study* (2021). It was only as I conducted research for this new book, following leads and threads into the 1970s, that I discovered Tough's seminal work and the research she undertook to articulate language development. For me and Julie, Tough's framework stands the test of time. It also poses a question:

What mental models do adults draw upon to formulate questions or provocations to support, connect or deepen learning in the EYFS?

Tough prompts us to think about the adult's role beyond asking a bunch of contextual questions at the point of learning. Again, do adults draw upon a framework to formulate precise questions or statements? (Please note, I have adapted the following quote from Tough's 1977 book *Talking and Learning* to remove the cultural bias of that time by changing the pronoun 'his' to the generic 'their'.)

'What are the choices we can make in attempting to help the child play [their] part in dialogue, and so promote [their] thinking and [their] use of language?' *Tough, 1977a*

Tough presents a connected and longitudinal classification of language; a way of describing how children select, organise and integrate language. Her toolkit helps us to classify the range of language that children are using and the cognitive demand or complexity.

From our work in the classroom, we know that this framework gives practitioners the skills and tools to dial into language development and begin to evaluate the child's choices. It also gives focus to adults' understanding of which strategies and opportunities the children need more of.

This framework and associated strategies to monitor (check) and evaluate (look for the value) spotlight our attention on how well children are using language and provide opportunities for language development.

Progression in language: the framework

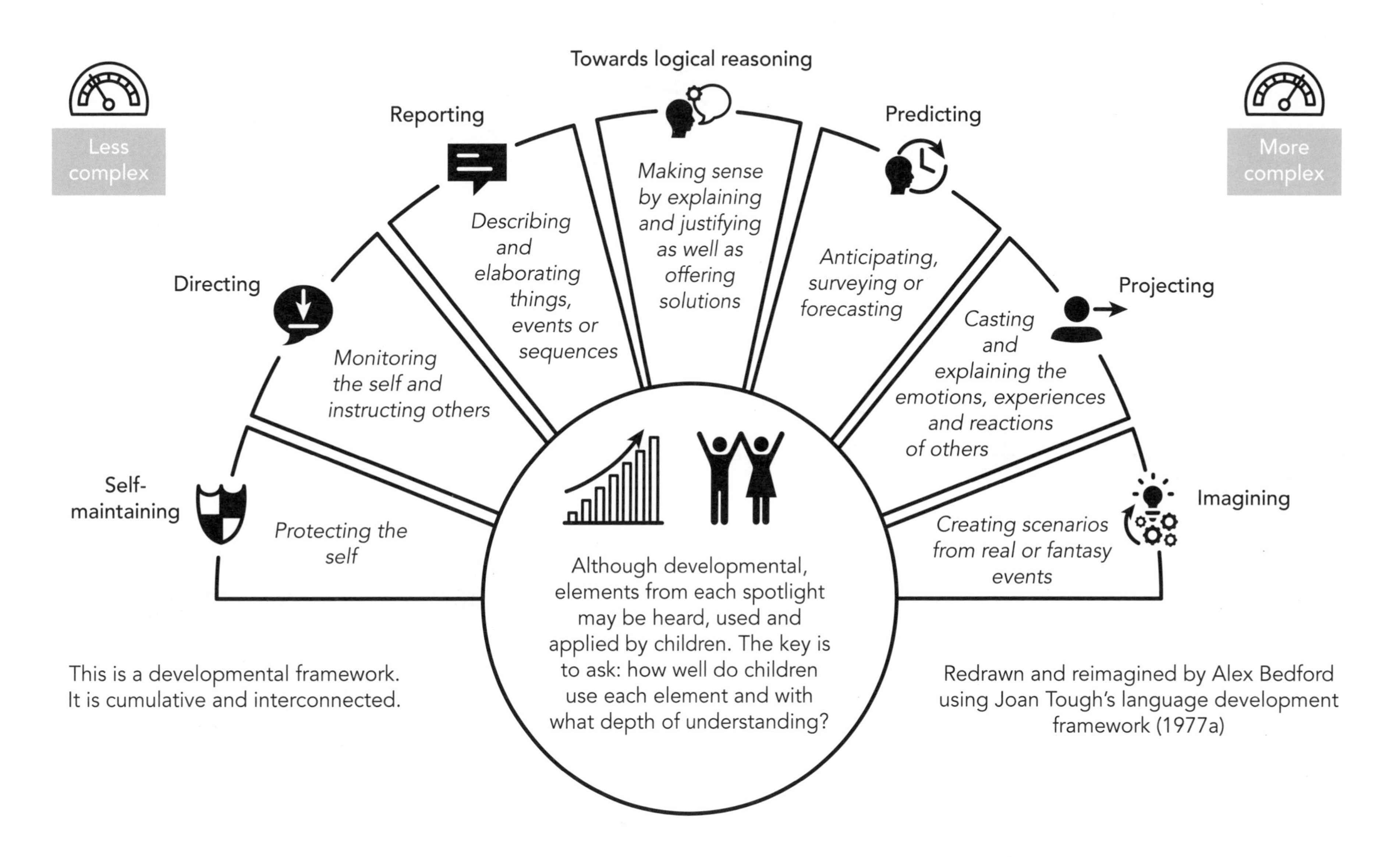

The ShREC approach

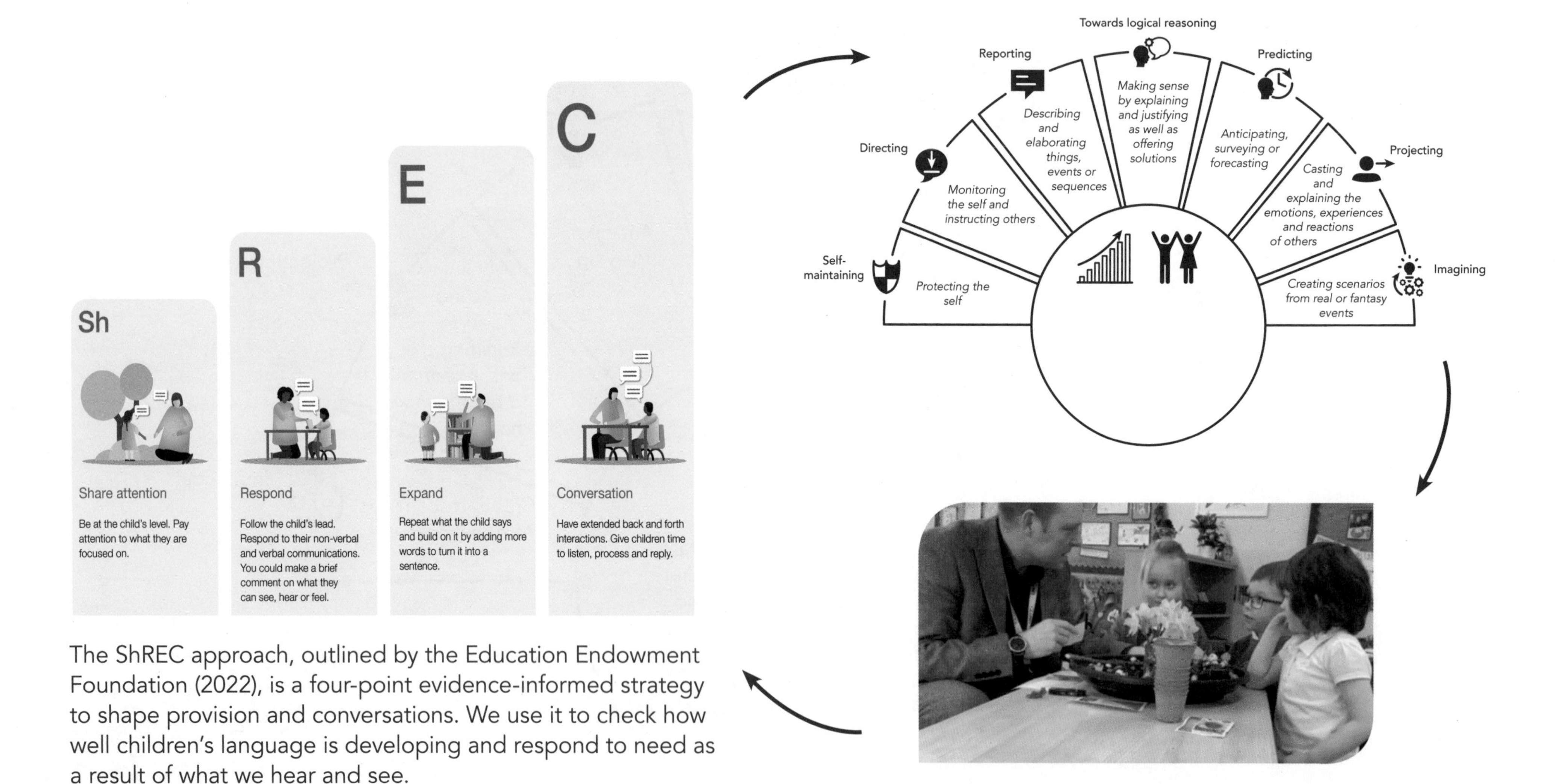

The ShREC approach, outlined by the Education Endowment Foundation (2022), is a four-point evidence-informed strategy to shape provision and conversations. We use it to check how well children's language is developing and respond to need as a result of what we hear and see.

Using the framework to be strategic and responsive

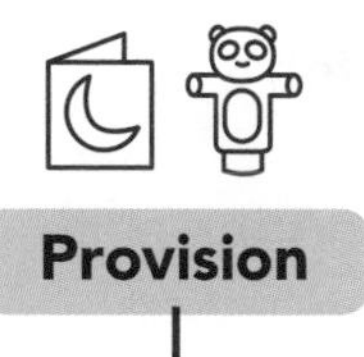

Provision

Planned resources to connect, inspire and structure planned learning opportunities

What provision do children need to support language development? How do you know?

Opportunity

Strategic long-term sequence to ensure coherent and cumulative progression

Consider the strategic and long-term nature of language development. Where do you precisely plan for these opportunities to happen?

Experience

Attention and engagement with tasks to develop understanding and help children to make sense of the provision

What activities will support and develop children's acquisition and use of language? Do the activities generate learning and long-term memory?

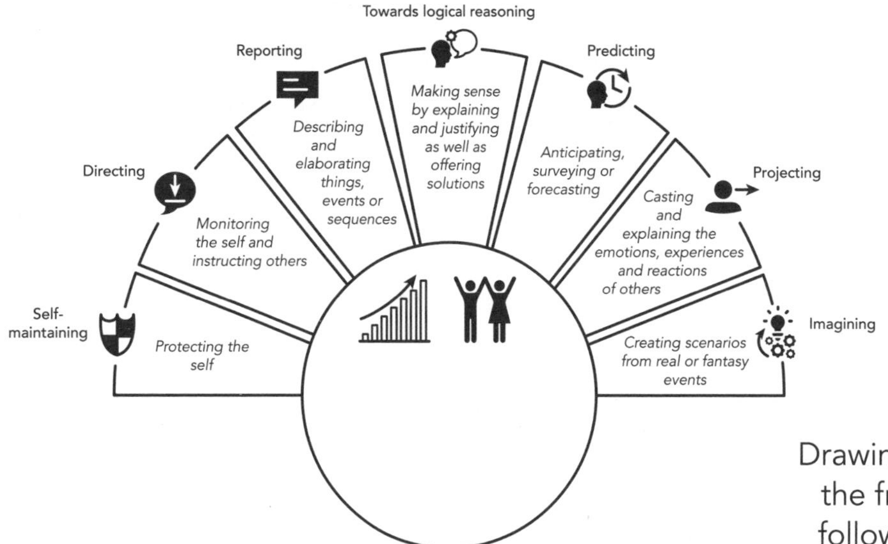

Drawing on Tough's research, we exemplify the framework's seven spotlights over the following pages, in the context of today…

The functions of language

More complex

Interpretive function

The reflection of the meaning the child has made from the opportunities, provision and experiences

Directive function

The organisation and implementation of physical actions

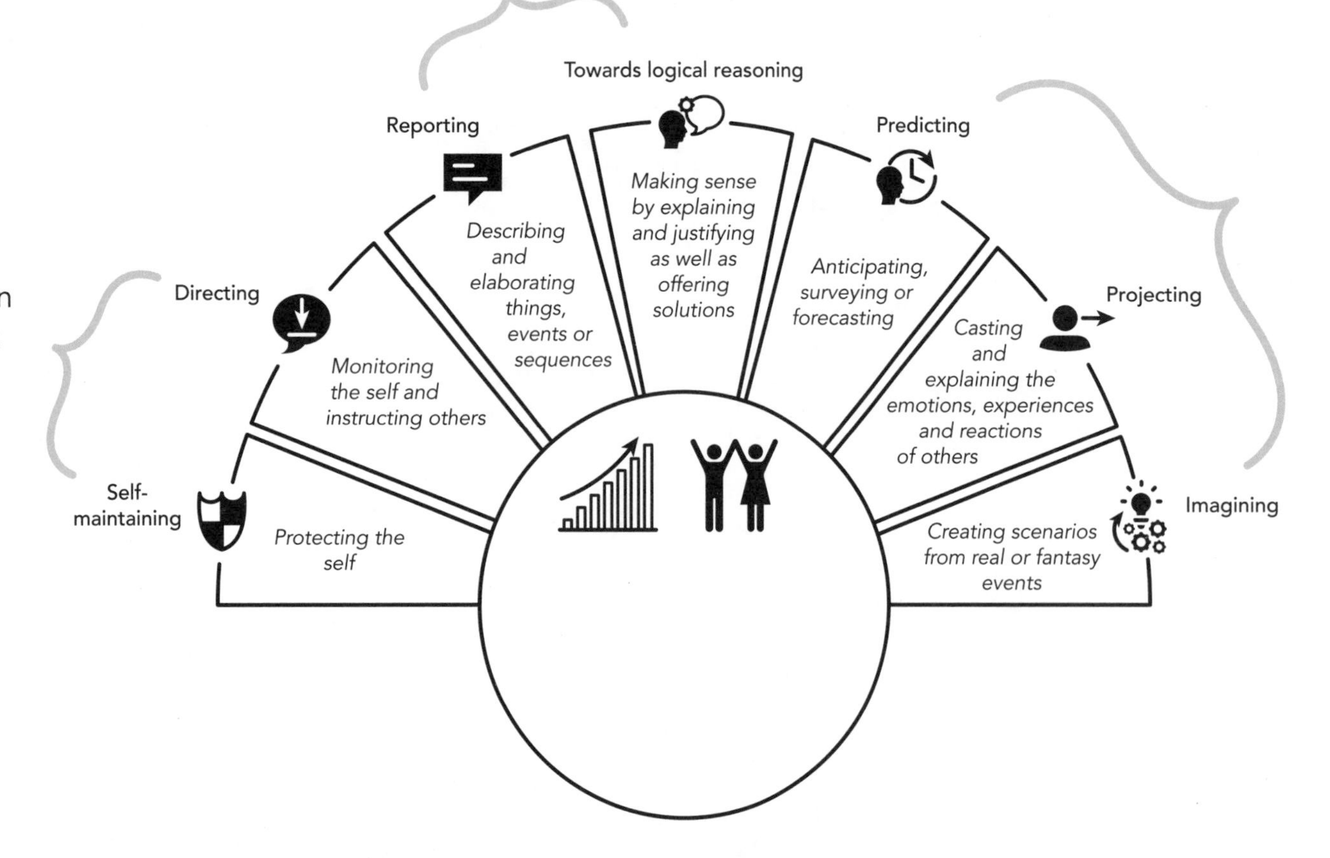

Projective function

The organisation of meaning for events that have not yet happened or may never take place at all

Self-maintaining

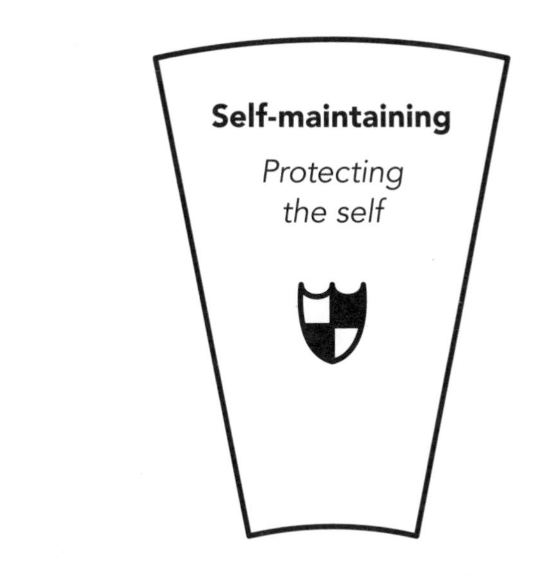

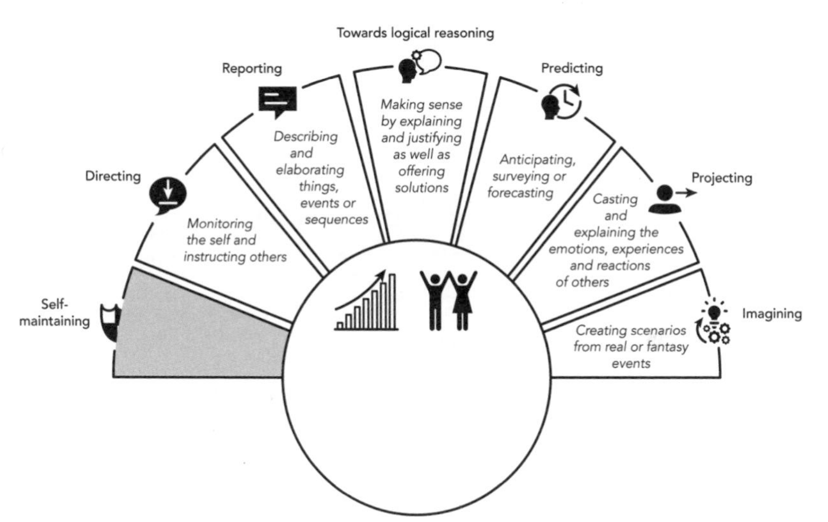

Psychological or physical needs	*'I'm thirsty.'* *'I want a hug.'*
Protect the self	*'Stop it.'* *'Go away.'*
Protect self-interests	*'It's mine.'* *'I want that.'*
Justify behaviour	*'She took it.'* *'I wanted it.'*
Criticise others	*'That's bad.'* *'I don't like it.'*
Threaten others	*'I'm the bad guy [rearing up in the faces of other children]...'* *'I'll hurt you...'*

Directing

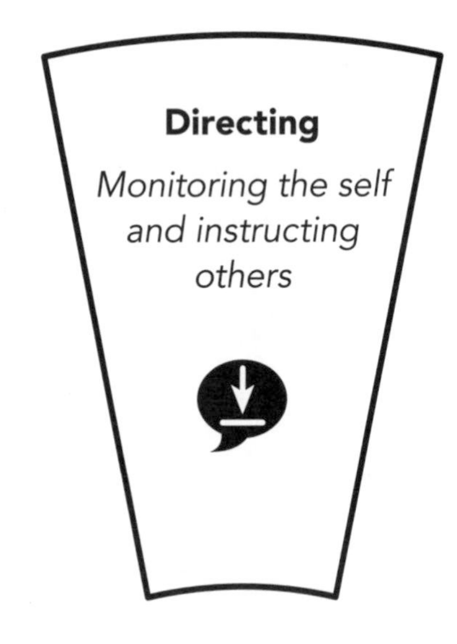

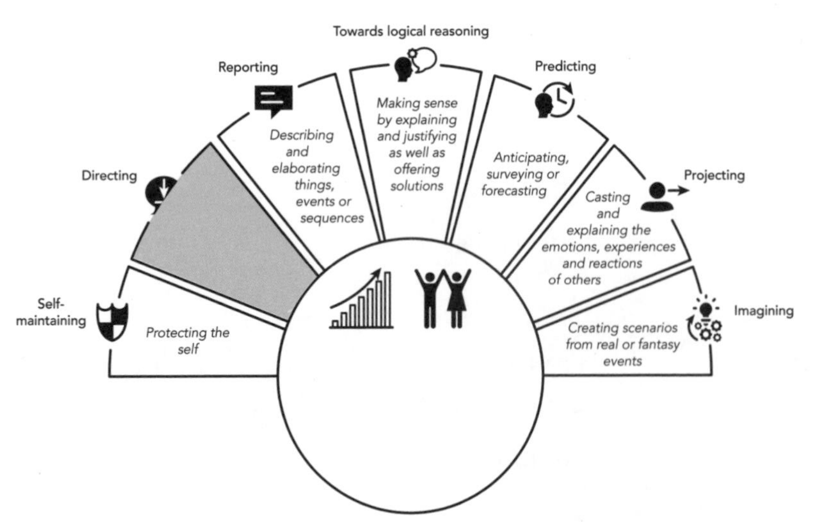

Monitor own actions

Language accompanies the child's actions – a running commentary of events as a monitoring strategy.

Self-direction (monitoring)

Focusing attention, e.g. the child is trying to get a lid off a jar:

'The – lid – is – too – tightly – put – on… I – will – turn – it.'

Direct own actions

'Put this brick on here…'

'Take this hat and you [talking to a teddy bear] can have this one.'

Direct the actions of others

Demonstration of actions.

Forward-planning to achieve a goal.

'You push that…'

'I just need to put this block down here.'

Collaborate in action with others

'Let's put this here…'

'You put that there…I'll hold the stick.'

Reporting

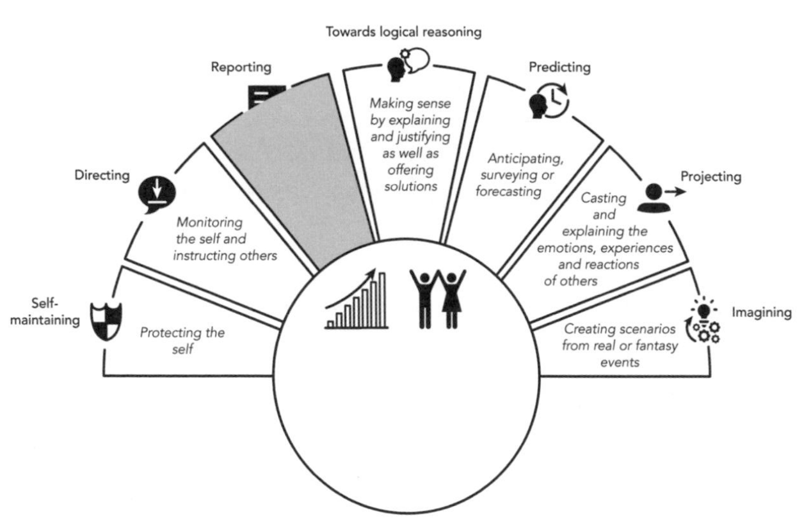

Label the component parts of a scene

Adult: 'Tell me, what's here? [pointing at a scene in the book Tad by Benji Davies]'

Child: 'Here is the pond and there is Tad. She is a tadpole.'

Elaborate and refer to detail: the colour, shape, size or position of an object

'Describe this to me [pointing to the frog image].'

'The little tadpole was in the pond.'

'The water looks cold.'

Talk about an incident

'Tell me, what happened to the frog?'

'The frogs jumped out of the pond.'

Absence of conditions

'A frog can't jump without legs [looking at a tadpole].'

Refer to a sequence of events

'So, Tad was scared of Big Blub. What happened next?'

'Tad hid in the weeds.'

Reflect on the meanings of experiences, including feelings

'How did you feel when…?'

'I felt scared when Tad was chased by Big Blub.'

Recognition of incongruity

'I think Big Blub is too big for the pond.'

Association with earlier experiences

'I've seen tadpoles in the pond. They were teeny-tiny.'

Towards logical reasoning

Towards logical reasoning

Making sense by explaining and justifying as well as offering solutions

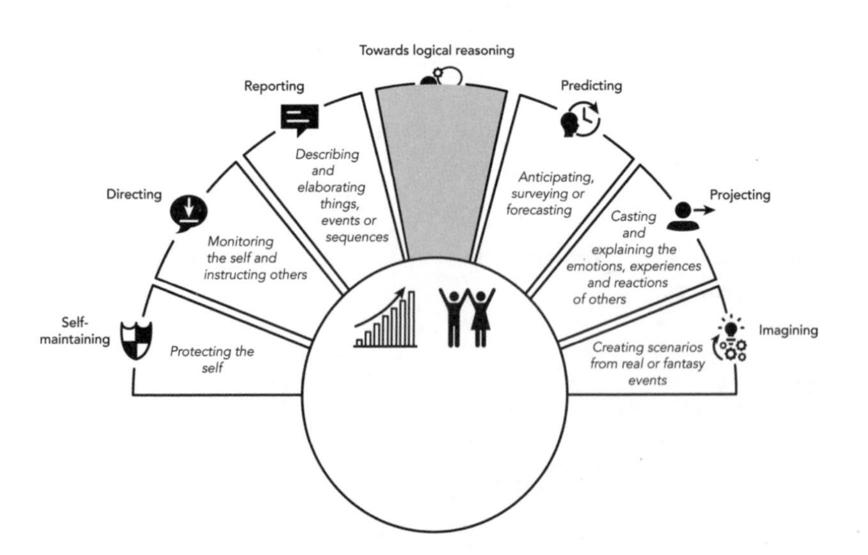

Explain a process

'I'm wondering, how do you make the colour orange?'

'You mix red and yellow paint to make orange.'

Recognise casual and dependent relationships

'What would you do to make that pancake taste sweeter?'

'You have to put sugar on the pancake.'

Recognise problems and solutions

'Why did Cyril want to store nuts for the winter?'

'What problem did Cyril have?'

(*The Squirrels Who Squabbled* by Rachel Bright and Jim Field)

'He wanted nuts to eat in the winter.'

'Cyril wanted the last pine cone, but Bruce wanted it too!'

Justify judgements and actions

'What would you do if there wasn't a space at the pine cone table?'

'I really wanted a go, so I waited until there was a space.'

Reflect on events and draw conclusions

'What good things happened when Cyril and Bruce worked as a team?'

'It was good that Cyril and Bruce helped each other. That way, they got to share the pine cones.'

Predicting

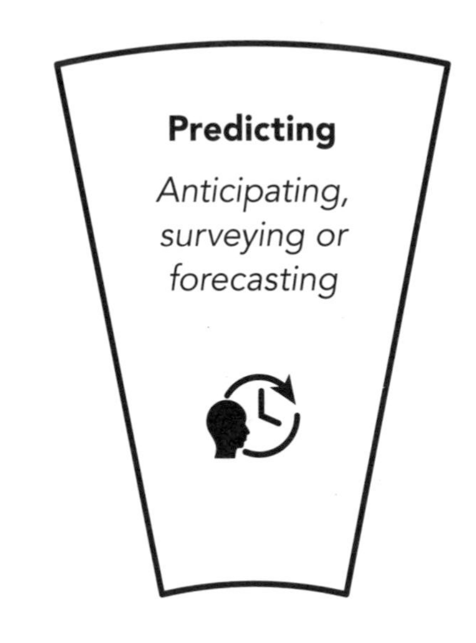

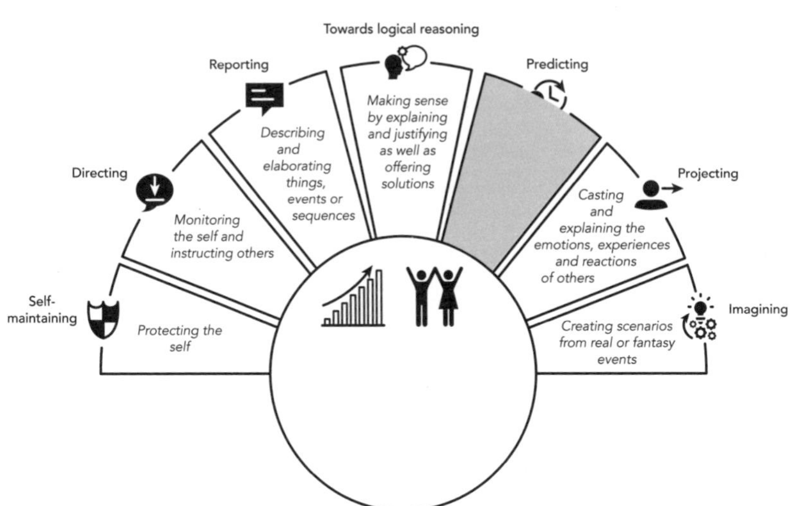

Anticipate or forecast events

'I wonder what happens when it is both sunny and rainy?'

'I think there will be a rainbow because it is sunny and rainy.'

Anticipate the detail and sequence of events

'What happens when Cyril, the squirrel, finds a nut?'

'The squirrel hides the nut by digging a hole. He buries it in the ground.'

Anticipate or predict the consequences of actions and events

'I'm going to put this in here. What do you think will happen?'

'Don't put the paint in there – it will make the sand too sticky and we won't be able to use it.'

Survey for possible alternatives

'If Tad swims quickly, he might escape from Big Blub.'

'I'd like a frog, but I think we'll get a cat first.'

Recognition of problems and prediction of solutions

'There's not enough water in the bowl, we'll have to get a jug to fill it up.'

'The frog puppet is wet, we'll have to dry it. I'll put it in the sun.'

Projecting

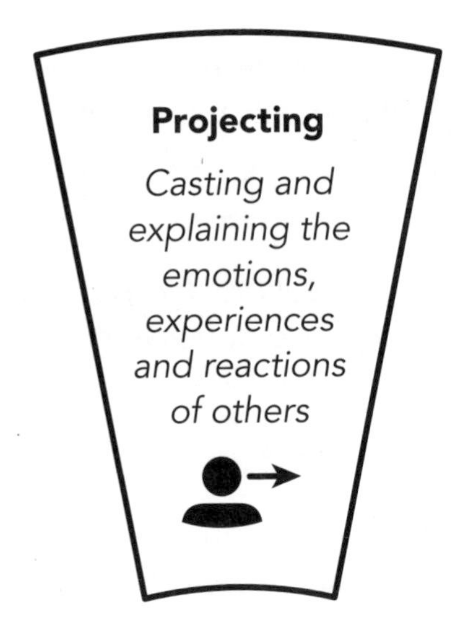

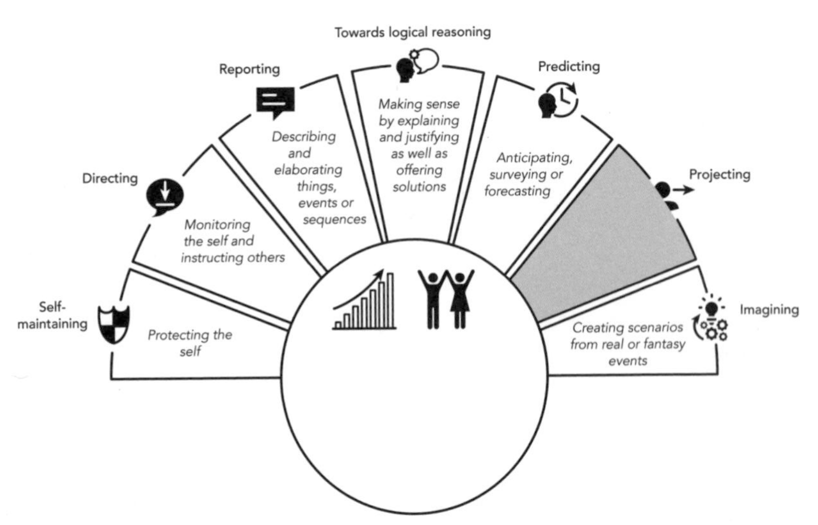

Project into the experiences of others

'Tell me, why do you think the bear chased the children?'

(*We're Going On a Bear Hunt* by Michael Rosen and Helen Oxenbury)

'He chased the children because they had woken him up.'

Project into the feelings of others

'Why do you think Isobel was sad?'

(*The Invisible* by Tom Percival)

'Isobel was sad because she had to leave her home. She had a happy home.'

Project into the reactions of others

'Why did Luna say "Hey!" to Finn?'

(*Luna Loves Art* by Joseph Coelho and Fiona Lumbers)

'Finn scrunched up her picture. He was cross. Luna was sad.'

Project into a situation never experienced

'If you were the turtle, how would you feel?'

'Why did Rocket get everyone to clean up the beach?'

(*Clean Up* by Nathan Bryon and Dapo Adeola)

'I would feel scared because I don't know if Rocket would hurt me.'

'Rocket wanted to help all the animals. There was lots of rubbish. It was a big job so she needed help.'

Imagining

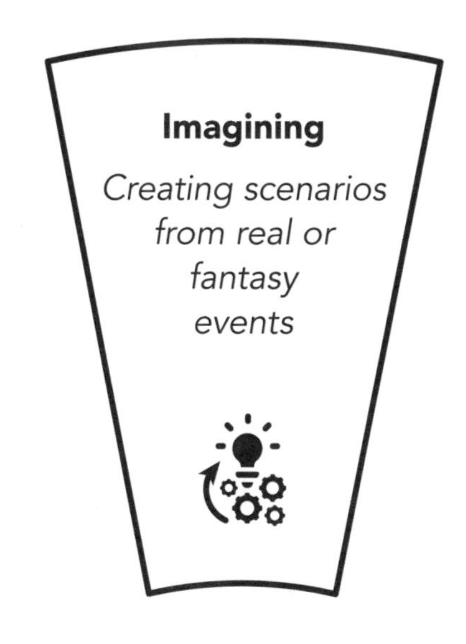

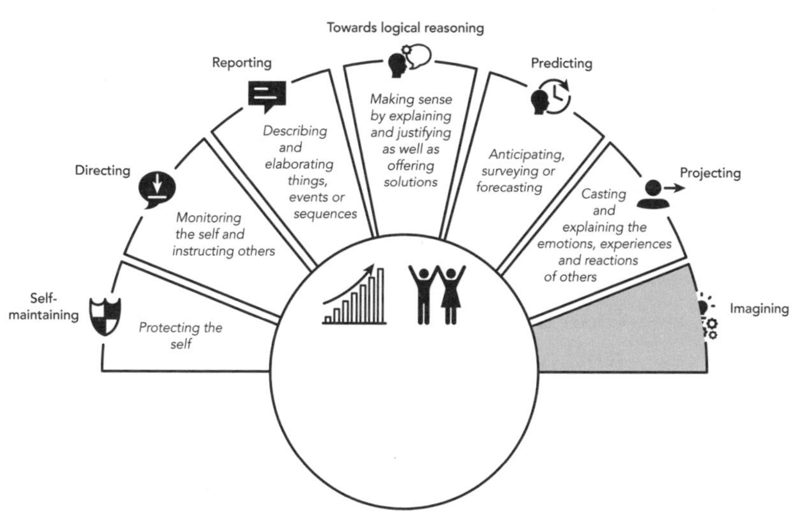

Develop an imagined situation based on real life

Language can be used to give commentary on the imaginary context of the child's play.

Resources can be used to represent the imagined play, but words then extend the meaning of the imagined scene.

'I'm Chet [the class guinea pig]. I'm hungry [covering Chet with a blanket]. Squeak, squeak. Please feed me...'

Develop an imagined situation based on fantasy

'Hello, it's the Martian here and I'm stuck on the Moon. The boy left me here all alone.'

(*The Way Back Home* by Oliver Jeffers)

'Hello, this is Space Rescue. Do you need help?'

'We will look for the boy and come to rescue you.'

'Let's get the tools, we're going to mend the Martian's space ship. I need a spanner...'

Strategic questions for EYFS settings

- *When do you hear and see pupils using this range of strategies?*
- *Is this built into the provision?*
- *Do pupils get high-quality explanations and worked examples via modelling with and to them?*

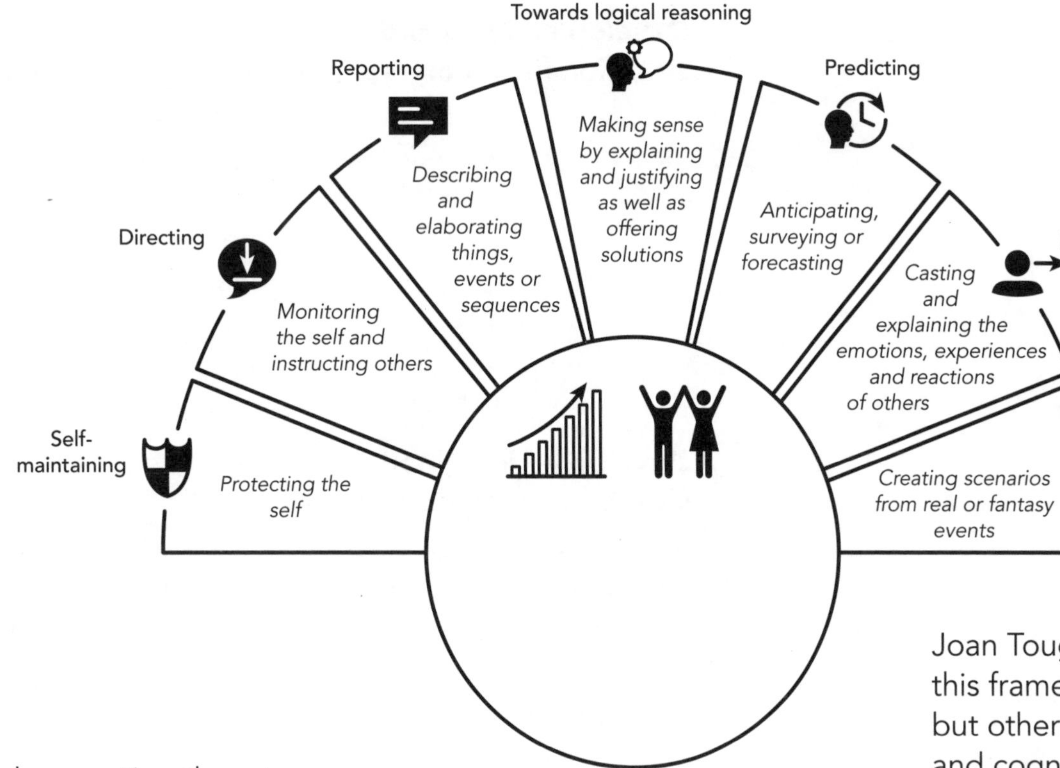

- *What opportunities do pupils have to attempt and apply these strategies?*
- *Are the more complex strategies accessible? Do they connect with prior experiences?*

Listening to children and prompting them to talk about prior or current experiences gives us a valuable insight into how they use and deploy language strategies. Providing children with meaningful and purposeful opportunities to use language is central to great learning in the EYFS.

Joan Tough recognised that some elements of this framework would be used by all children, but others would not use the more complex and cognitively challenging strategies.

> ***'...many children seem to do no more than use words to place labels on objects and actions; they are not disposed to be analytical and do not use more complex strategies of reporting'***
>
> *Tough, 1977a*

Worked examples using the seven spotlights of language development

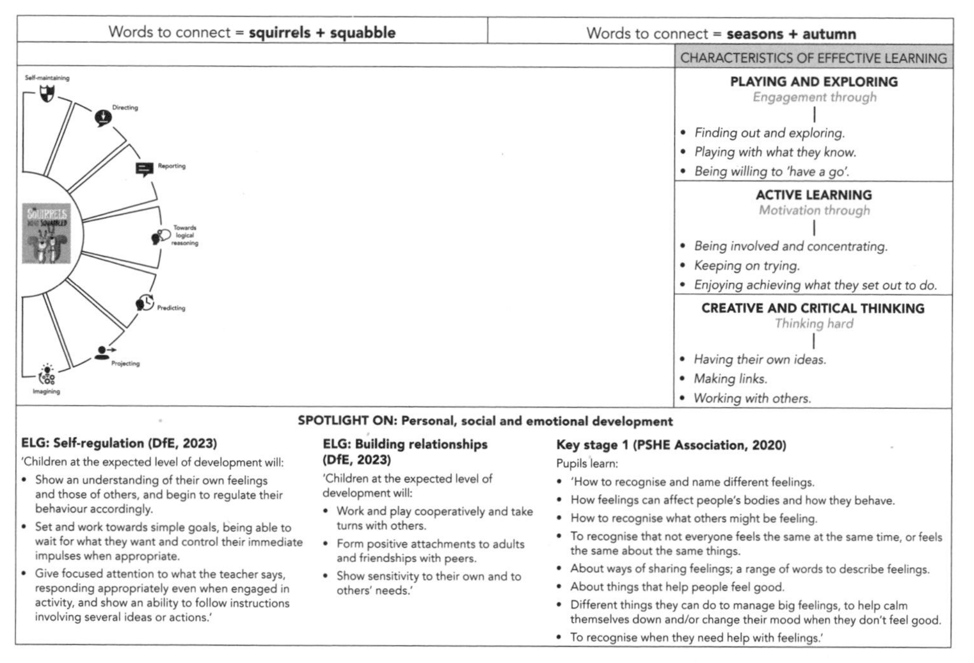
Words to connect = **squirrels + squabble** | Words to connect = **seasons + autumn**

CHARACTERISTICS OF EFFECTIVE LEARNING

PLAYING AND EXPLORING
Engagement through
- *Finding out and exploring.*
- *Playing with what they know.*
- *Being willing to 'have a go'.*

ACTIVE LEARNING
Motivation through
- *Being involved and concentrating.*
- *Keeping on trying.*
- *Enjoying achieving what they set out to do.*

CREATIVE AND CRITICAL THINKING
Thinking hard
- *Having their own ideas.*
- *Making links.*
- *Working with others.*

SPOTLIGHT ON: Personal, social and emotional development

ELG: Self-regulation (DfE, 2023)
'Children at the expected level of development will:
- Show an understanding of their own feelings and those of others, and begin to regulate their behaviour accordingly.
- Set and work towards simple goals, being able to wait for what they want and control their immediate impulses when appropriate.
- Give focused attention to what the teacher says, responding appropriately even when engaged in activity, and show an ability to follow instructions involving several ideas or actions.'

ELG: Building relationships (DfE, 2023)
'Children at the expected level of development will:
- Work and play cooperatively and take turns with others.
- Form positive attachments to adults and friendships with peers.
- Show sensitivity to their own and to others' needs.'

Key stage 1 (PSHE Association, 2020)
Pupils learn:
- 'How to recognise and name different feelings.
- How feelings can affect people's bodies and how they behave.
- How to recognise what others might be feeling.
- To recognise that not everyone feels the same at the same time, or feels the same about the same things.
- About ways of sharing feelings; a range of words to describe feelings.
- About things that help people feel good.
- Different things they can do to manage big feelings, to help calm themselves down and/or change their mood when they don't feel good.
- To recognise when they need help with feelings.'

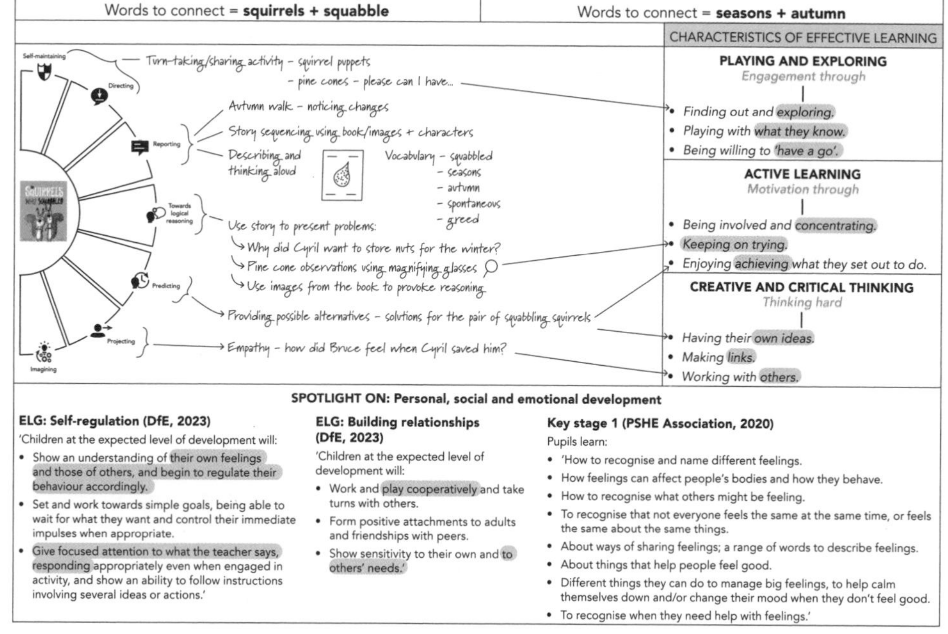
Words to connect = **squirrels + squabble** | Words to connect = **seasons + autumn**

CHARACTERISTICS OF EFFECTIVE LEARNING

PLAYING AND EXPLORING
Engagement through
- *Finding out and exploring.*
- *Playing with what they know.*
- *Being willing to 'have a go'.*

ACTIVE LEARNING
Motivation through
- *Being involved and concentrating.*
- *Keeping on trying.*
- *Enjoying achieving what they set out to do.*

CREATIVE AND CRITICAL THINKING
Thinking hard
- *Having their own ideas.*
- *Making links.*
- *Working with others.*

SPOTLIGHT ON: Personal, social and emotional development

ELG: Self-regulation (DfE, 2023)
'Children at the expected level of development will:
- Show an understanding of their own feelings and those of others, and begin to regulate their behaviour accordingly.
- Set and work towards simple goals, being able to wait for what they want and control their immediate impulses when appropriate.
- Give focused attention to what the teacher says, responding appropriately even when engaged in activity, and show an ability to follow instructions involving several ideas or actions.'

ELG: Building relationships (DfE, 2023)
'Children at the expected level of development will:
- Work and play cooperatively and take turns with others.
- Form positive attachments to adults and friendships with peers.
- Show sensitivity to their own and to others' needs.'

Key stage 1 (PSHE Association, 2020)
Pupils learn:
- 'How to recognise and name different feelings.
- How feelings can affect people's bodies and how they behave.
- How to recognise what others might be feeling.
- To recognise that not everyone feels the same at the same time, or feels the same about the same things.
- About ways of sharing feelings; a range of words to describe feelings.
- About things that help people feel good.
- Different things they can do to manage big feelings, to help calm themselves down and/or change their mood when they don't feel good.
- To recognise when they need help with feelings.'

We've written extensive worked examples in Chapter 5 that act as a simple planning toolkit to focus provision and learning experiences around the development of language. The examples are usually inspired by a particular book or provision.

We decided to focus on the interpretive (reporting and towards logical reasoning) and projective (predicting, projecting and imagining) functions of language through structured and deliberate conversations that align beautifully with the importance of dialogue and oracy.

When observing and interacting with children at the point of provision, the first two spotlights within the directive function (self-monitoring and directing) are clear to see. As a result, we don't include these in the sustained shared thinking conversations.

On the following pages is a sample worked example based on *The Squirrels Who Squabbled* by Rachel Bright and Jim Field.

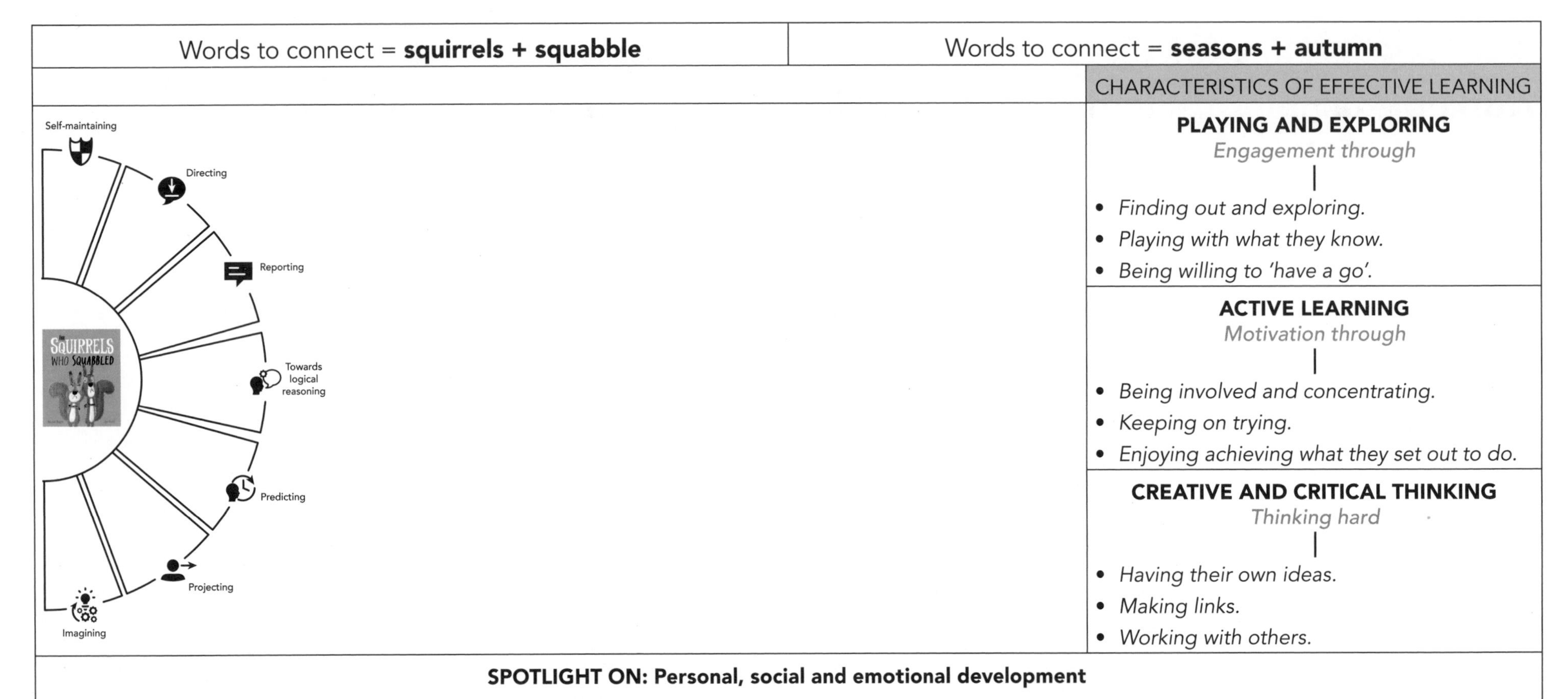

SPOTLIGHT ON: Personal, social and emotional development

ELG: Self-regulation (DfE, 2023)

'Children at the expected level of development will:

- Show an understanding of their own feelings and those of others, and begin to regulate their behaviour accordingly.
- Set and work towards simple goals, being able to wait for what they want and control their immediate impulses when appropriate.
- Give focused attention to what the teacher says, responding appropriately even when engaged in activity, and show an ability to follow instructions involving several ideas or actions.'

ELG: Building relationships (DfE, 2023)

'Children at the expected level of development will:

- Work and play cooperatively and take turns with others.
- Form positive attachments to adults and friendships with peers.
- Show sensitivity to their own and to others' needs.'

Key stage 1 (PSHE Association, 2020)

Pupils learn:

- 'How to recognise and name different feelings.
- How feelings can affect people's bodies and how they behave.
- How to recognise what others might be feeling.
- To recognise that not everyone feels the same at the same time, or feels the same about the same things.
- About ways of sharing feelings; a range of words to describe feelings.
- About things that help people feel good.
- Different things they can do to manage big feelings, to help calm themselves down and/or change their mood when they don't feel good.
- To recognise when they need help with feelings.'

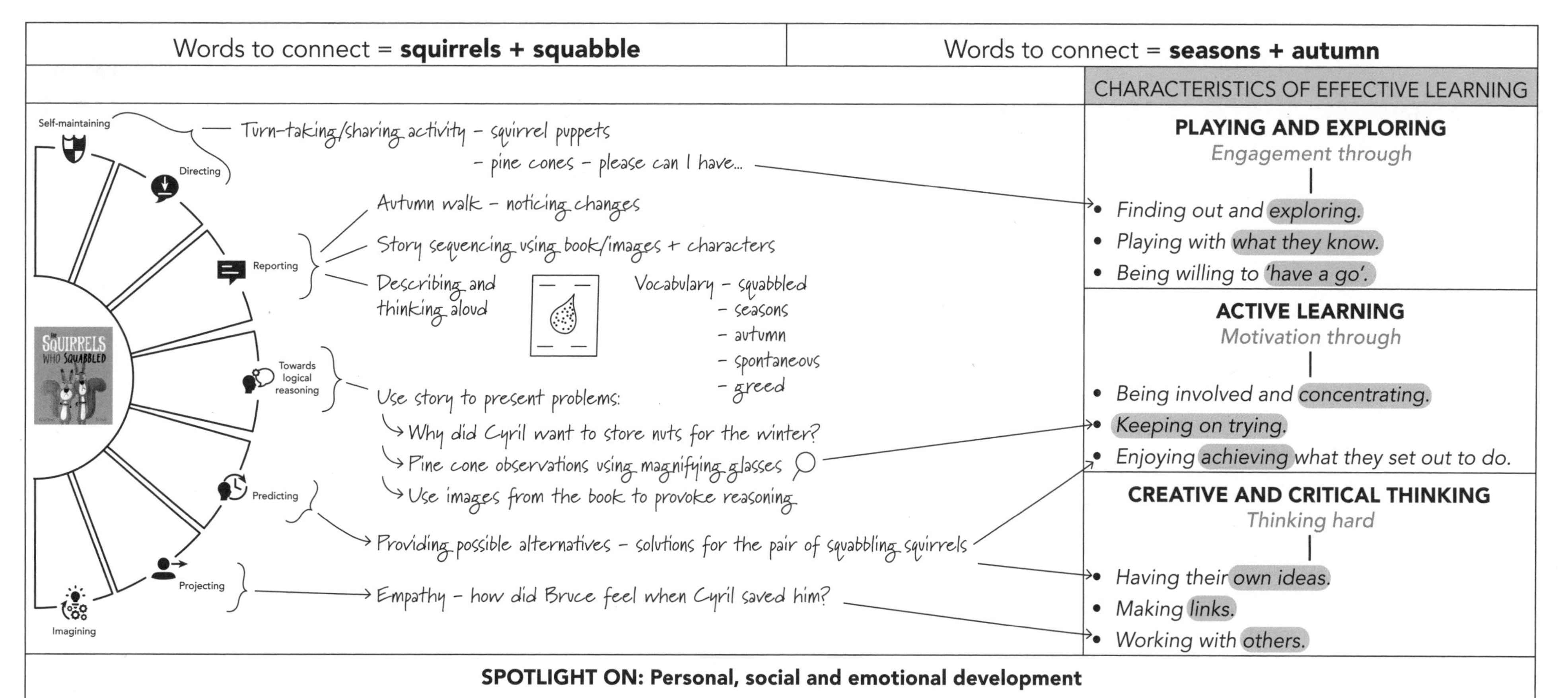

SPOTLIGHT ON: Personal, social and emotional development

ELG: Self-regulation (DfE, 2023)

'Children at the expected level of development will:

- Show an understanding of their own feelings and those of others, and begin to regulate their behaviour accordingly.
- Set and work towards simple goals, being able to wait for what they want and control their immediate impulses when appropriate.
- Give focused attention to what the teacher says, responding appropriately even when engaged in activity, and show an ability to follow instructions involving several ideas or actions.'

ELG: Building relationships (DfE, 2023)

'Children at the expected level of development will:

- Work and play cooperatively and take turns with others.
- Form positive attachments to adults and friendships with peers.
- Show sensitivity to their own and to others' needs.'

Key stage 1 (PSHE Association, 2020)

Pupils learn:

- 'How to recognise and name different feelings.
- How feelings can affect people's bodies and how they behave.
- How to recognise what others might be feeling.
- To recognise that not everyone feels the same at the same time, or feels the same about the same things.
- About ways of sharing feelings; a range of words to describe feelings.
- About things that help people feel good.
- Different things they can do to manage big feelings, to help calm themselves down and/or change their mood when they don't feel good.
- To recognise when they need help with feelings.'

Questions to check language development and understanding

 Reporting	Towards logical reasoning	 Predicting	Projecting	Imagining
Identify the components of the images or book | *'What do you see on this page?'* **Refer to detail: the colour and shape, size or position of an object** | *'Describe this [pointing at pine cone].'* **Elaboration** **Identify and describe images or scenes from the book** | *'Tell me, what happens when Cyril finds the pine cone?'* **Talk about a sequence of events** | *'What are the seasons?'* **Absence of conditions** | *'Why was the pine cone so precious to Cyril?'*	**Explain a process** | *'How did Cyril and Bruce get ready for the long winter months?'* **Recognise casual and dependent relationships** | *'How did the pine cone bring Cyril and Bruce together?'* *'How do the words "squirrel" and "squabble" connect?'* **Recognise problems and causes** | *'What problem did Cyril and Bruce have?'* **Justify judgements and actions** | *'Was Bruce right to take the pine cone away from Cyril?'*	**Anticipate or forecast** | *'Bruce was getting ready to store his food for the winter. Why was he doing that?'* **Predict the consequences of actions and events** | *'When Cyril and Bruce squabbled, how do you think they felt?'* *'How did they feel afterwards?'* *'If the pine cone was lost, what could have happened to the squirrels?'* **Survey for possible alternatives** | *'What other solutions could Cyril and Bruce come up with? What would you do?'*	**Project into the experiences, feelings and reactions of others** | *'Tell me, why did the squirrels squabble about the pine cone?'* *'When they were squabbling, how do you think Bruce felt?'* *'When the squirrels had made friends, how do you think Cyril felt?'* **Reflect on the meaning of experiences** | *'How did you feel when Cyril and Bruce argued?'* **Project into a situation never experienced** | *'If you were Bruce, how would you have stopped the squabbling?'*	**In an imagined context** | Using puppets, characters or a phone or walkie-talkie.    *'Hello, Bruce, this is the pine cone shop. How many pine cones would you like?'* *'Hello, Cyril, this is the pine cone bank. Why do you want to keep so many pine cones?'*

Ask yourself...

If you were asked these questions, how would you answer?

1. When reflecting on your own practice and setting, what stands out for you around the seven spotlights of language development?
2. How do you see the seven spotlights supporting you to secure excellence in language development?
3. How will the seven spotlights help to bring consistency and precision questioning into your setting? How do they link to the work you may have already undertaken on language development (e.g. ShREC approach/early language screeners/intervention)?
4. What further staff training would you need to secure excellence in communication and language development across your setting?
5. How could you use the seven spotlights to support parents as partners, to shape coherent provision, and to build an understanding and love for language that spreads across and beyond the school community (e.g. to PVI settings and pre-schools)?

Chapter 3

Essential research for EYFS settings

Attention and perception

What's the difference?

Attention

Is the process of actively selecting and focusing on something at the expense of something else.

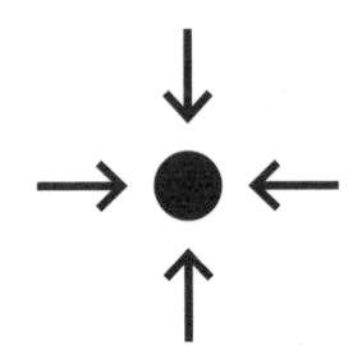

Perception

Is making sense of the information we receive from the provision and the learning environment.

The importance of routines

Peps Mccrea (2021) helps us to understand the importance of routines to focus attention on the content of learning.

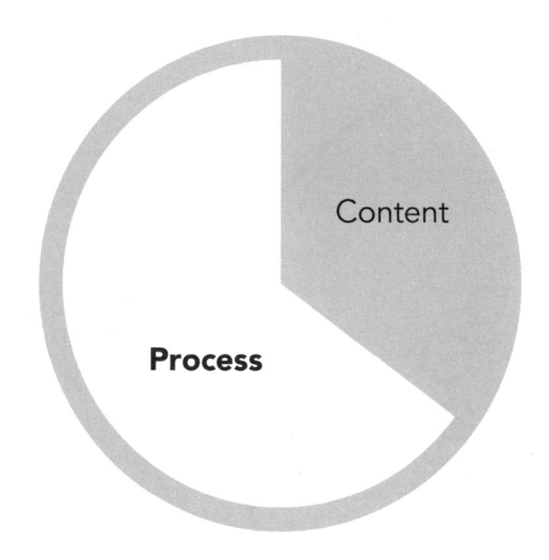

When an activity or expectation is not familiar or routine, the child's attention is focused on the process of doing. The content becomes a passenger and less attention is paid to it.

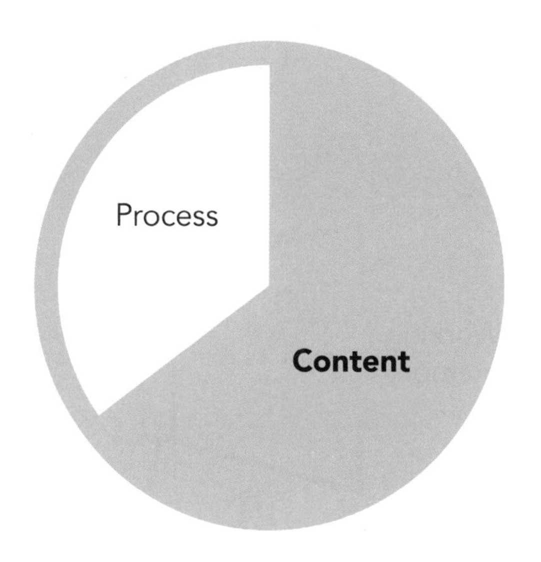

When an activity or expectation is known, practised and embedded, the process of doing becomes automatic and the content becomes the main focus of attention.

To embed routines and make them automatic, there are things we need to do:

Worked examples

My turn

'I'm going to show you...'

followed by

Shared practice

Our turn

'Let's do this together...'

followed by

Independent practice

Your turn

'Use what you know and can do...'

Working memory and long-term memory

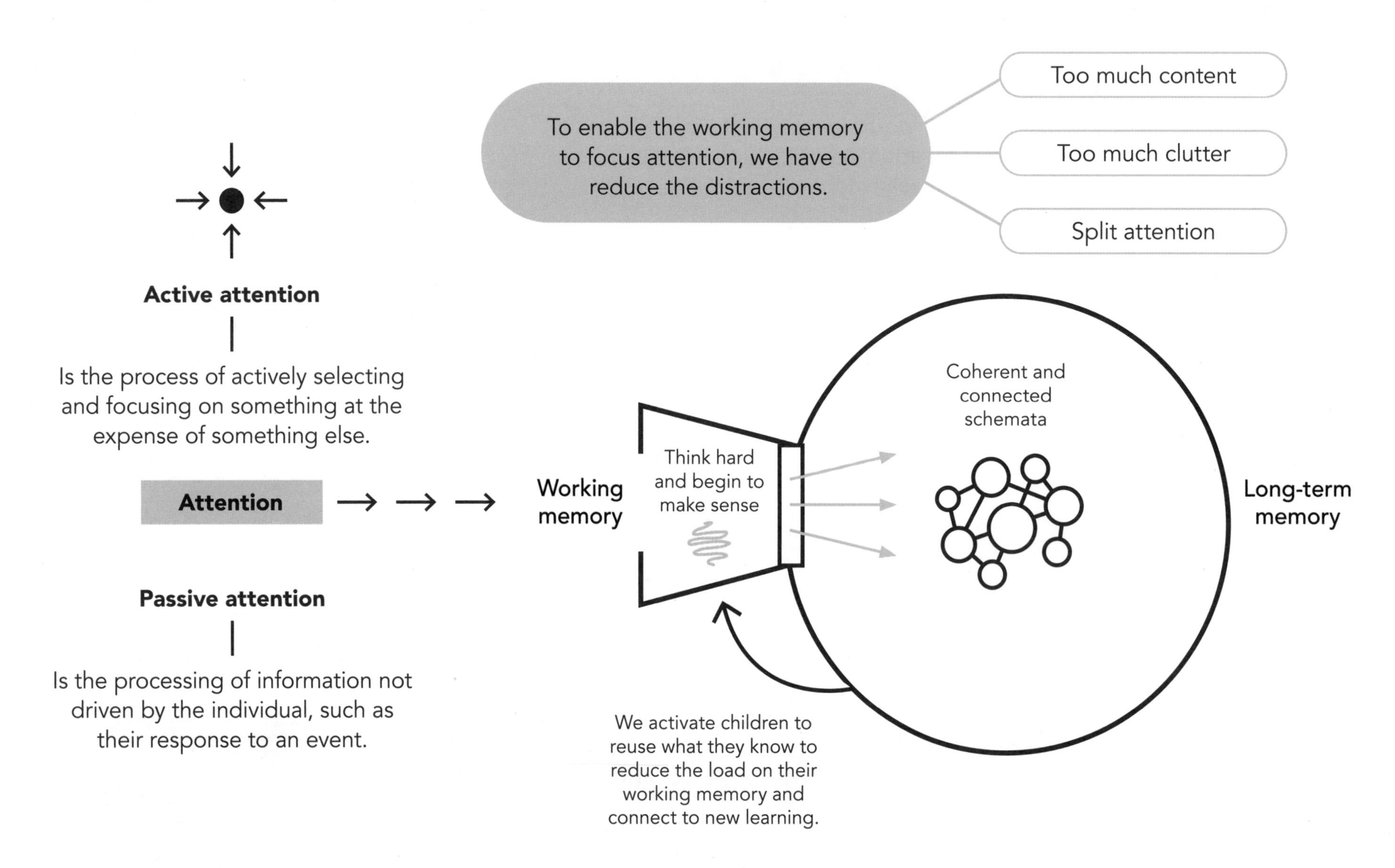

Working memory and long-term memory

The **working memory** is like a spotlight. If the spotlight of the working memory focuses on the intended learning and activity then active and desired learning can take place.

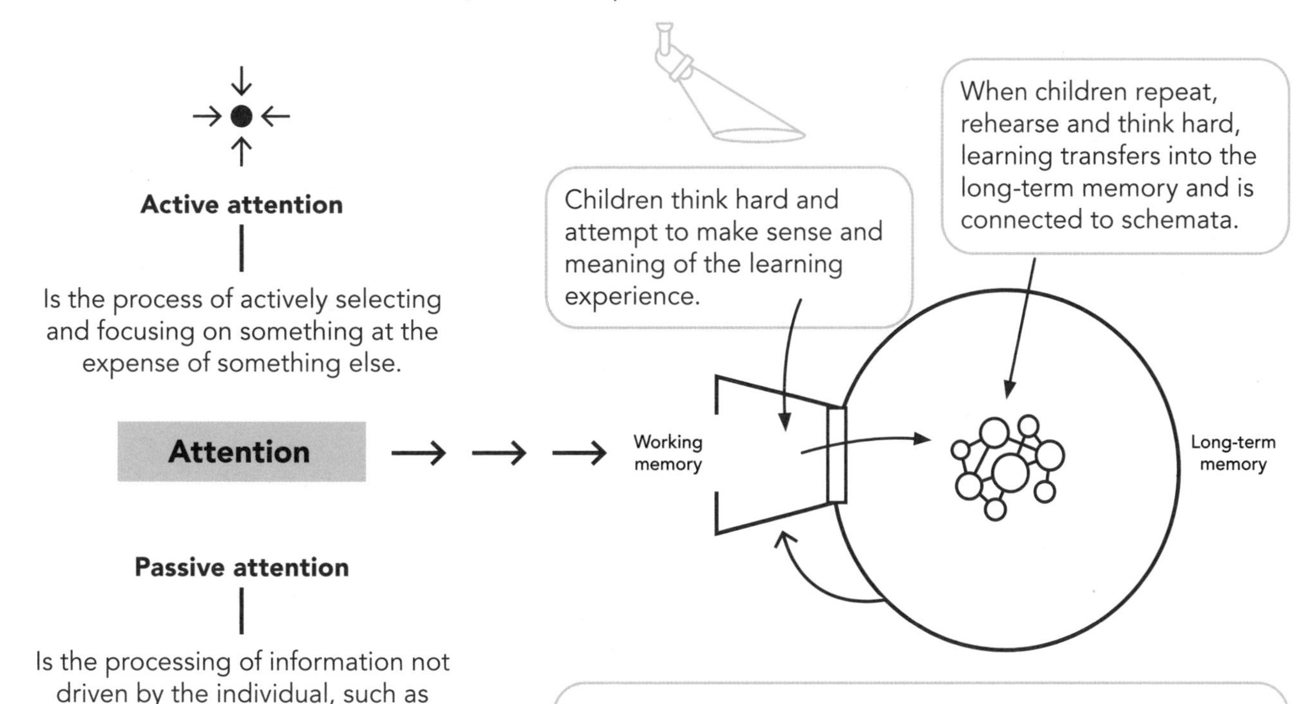

The **central executive**, or the executive function, is responsible for organising and coordinating cognition and thought through:

- Focusing attention on specific things.
- Dividing attention between events.
- Switching attention across tasks.
- Interacting with and integrating information in the long-term memory.

Learning is directly affected by **attention**. If the desired learning is not brought to the attention of the **working memory** then the intended learning is less likely to take place.

Children acquire, rehearse and think hard using vocabulary, resources and activities in order to process and make sense and meaning of the intended learning. Learning is modelled to children by an adult.

Cognitive routines such as spaced retrieval and deliberate practice

'Many children talk readily about the present scene but not all children draw frequently on their past experiences. Fostering a child's communication skills would include stimulating the child to recall [their] past experiences regularly, and to reflect on them and express [their] thinking about them'

Tough, 1977a

Drawing on the cognitive science of spaced retrieval practice and retrieval practice, strengthening the memory trace by revisiting prior experiences is a strategy in which young children need direction and provocation in order to perform.

This strategy is built into the teaching of early reading through phonics instruction – for example, in the only fully evaluated and research-focused methodology we champion, which is called Sounds-Write.

Routines and deliberate practice are part of the daily diet for young and emerging readers.

- How well are these cognitive strategies built into the prime and specific areas of the EYFS?
- How well do practitioners draw on the children's past experiences? Is this intentional?
- Do the design of the curriculum and its coherence provide opportunities to enrich and revisit prior content?
- What dialogue and spoken opportunities do children have to consciously remember and retrieve prior experiences?

Hermann Ebbinghaus' forgetting curve (1885)

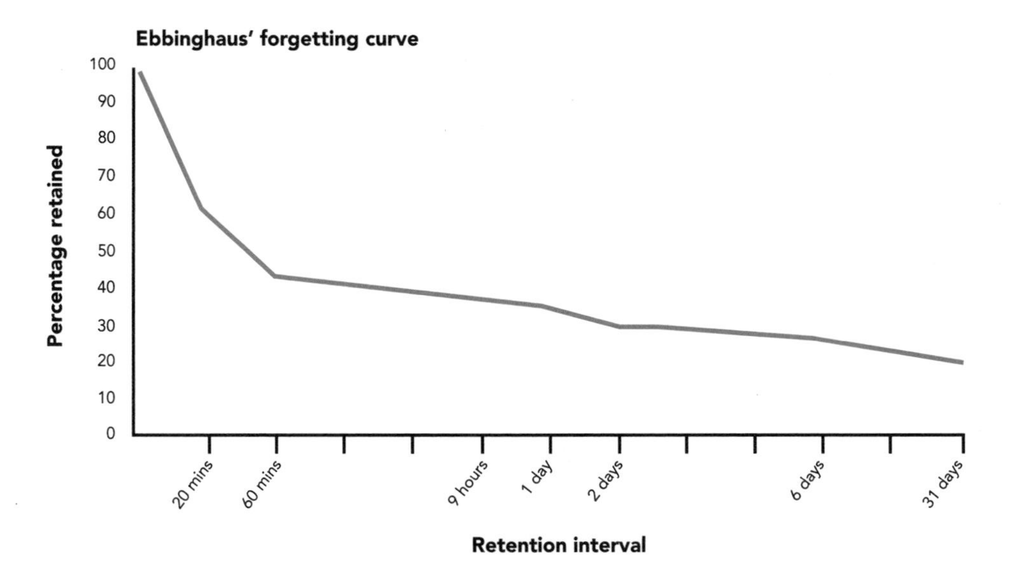

Remember, the brain places greater importance on repeated information.

Retrieval and spaced retrieval practice strengthen the memory trace and cognitive recall.

Strategically revisiting opportunities, provision and experiences will ease the forgetting curve and strengthen the memory trace, resulting in more efficient retrieval.

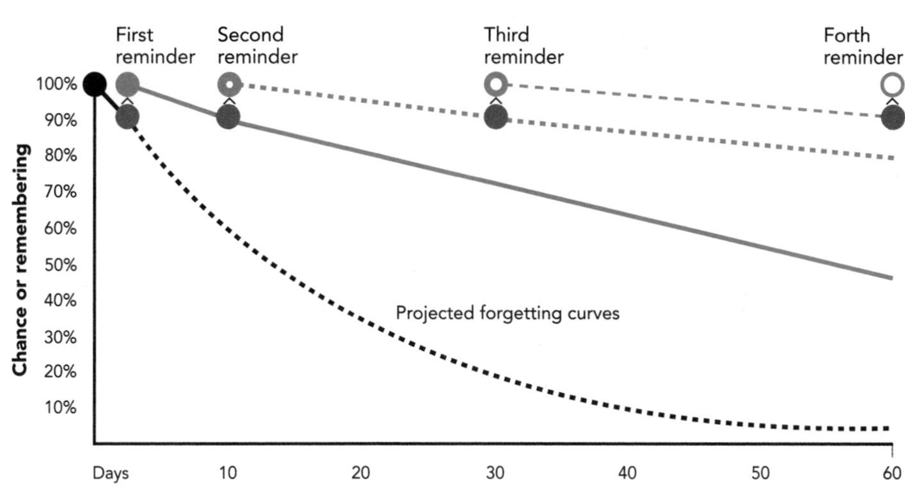

Attempting and applying

Deliberate practice: opportunity + provision + experience

To think hard, children need to engage in and attend to deliberate practice. That means they rehearse and use the knowledge they have acquired in order to become a little more expert. Opportunities for deliberate practice should be planned throughout your provision.

Deliberate practice is a low-threat developmental activity that increases in sophistication through adult interaction or provision. That makes the activity generative – learning is generated as a result.

Deliberate practice chunks complex learning into manageable small steps, so learning over time is cumulative and coherent. It is sequential and part of a broader learning sequence with increased cognitive demand, which results in children knowing more and being able to use that knowledge competently.

Children 'attempt and apply', using what they know to consolidate or sophisticate their understanding. Children's use and application of language is key to knowing how well they are developing their understanding.

Drawing on memory and using what you know

Retrieval practice

Frequently returning to content enables pupils to select, connect, remember, reuse, apply and integrate new knowledge. What has been instructed is retrieved though carefully planned provision and experiences; the children begin to make sense of the content through attempting, applying and challenging their understanding. Adults support retrieval through teacher-led, guided and independent activities.

John Walker and Tita Beaven articulate this brilliantly through their world-class evidence-informed phonics programme: Sounds-Write. Retrieval practice is integral to the systematic teaching (direct instruction) of phonics. Through Sounds-Write, we constantly and systematically (linked to assessment for learning) retrieve the GPCs that pupils already know/have been taught. Pupils then use this knowledge in order to blend to read new words. Children further apply this knowledge when reading matched decodables and spelling phonetically.

Retrieval should be cumulative and coherent. It should also be responsive, as we feed our formative assessments forward into the sequence of lessons.

Ask yourself...

Where would it be advantageous to plan systematic retrieval and deliberate practice focusing on foundational knowledge and vocabulary within your setting?

Revisiting and connecting prior learning to new learning

Spaced retrieval practice

Spaced retrieval practice involves strategically revisiting the content that children know and can use, so they have the opportunity to consolidate and elaborate the intended learning, as well as connecting it to new knowledge and experiences.

Planning learning as a long-term retrieval opportunity ensures the offer is coherent and cumulative. It also helps with strategic provision planning and enables us to think hard about the experiences children will encounter over a period of time.

Here's an example:
Say we want children to become a little better at making sense of their physical world and their community (EYFS educational programme).

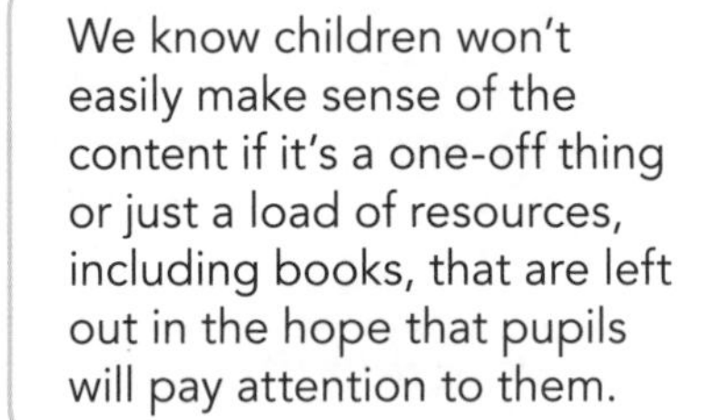

We know children won't easily make sense of the content if it's a one-off thing or just a load of resources, including books, that are left out in the hope that pupils will pay attention to them.

Be deliberate with your choices about where the attention is focused.

We want children to understand some important processes and changes in the natural world around them, including the seasons and changing states of matter (ELG).

You could take pupils on weekly walks, following the same route.

Make planned, clear and deliberate vocabulary choices, such as 'tree', 'leaf', 'autumn'…

Can children report what they hear and see? Do they select their vocabulary deliberately?

As the weekly walks routine becomes embedded, pupils will be better able to process the changing information and transfer what they know from receptive language stores to expressive language.

Make deliberate choices to progress children's use of language as the environments change over time. The route of the walk is the constant; the natural world is always changing.

See our worked example on page 47

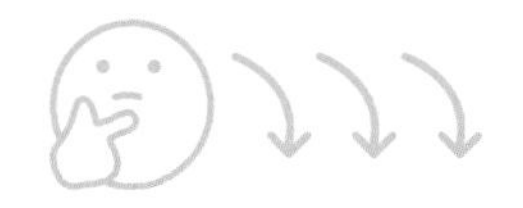

Spaced retrieval practice: worked example

These are the constants that thread through the provision. Children's understanding grows through the planned opportunities, provision and experiences.

- Route…
- Weather…
- Celebrations…
- Trees…
- Plants…
- Animals…
- Insects…

September
It is autumn. The trees all have leaves. There are plants and flowers. It is warm. It is sunny and can rain too.

October
It is autumn. Some leaves are starting to change colour. The weather changes – it is warm and cold. Christian people celebrate harvest. Jewish people celebrate Rosh Hashanah and Yom Kippur.

November
It is autumn. Some trees still have leaves, others have nearly lost them all. There are fewer insects and animals about. It is getting colder and stormier.

December
It is winter. The days are shorter. It is colder and stormier. Christians celebrate Christmas.

January
It is winter. It is cold.
Some trees have no leaves.
You won't see many insects at all.
Some plants have died back.
It is stormier – snow and frosts.
It is Chinese New Year.

February
It is winter. It is cold. Some trees still have no leaves. You can't see many insects. Some plants start to grow, like snowdrops.

March
It is spring: warmer. You may see some plants growing and pushing out of the ground. Trees grow leaves. Days get longer. Muslims fast for Ramadan.

April
It is spring. Some trees are growing leaves again. Other trees make blossom. There are more insects about. Christians celebrate Easter. Muslims celebrate Eid. Baby birds and animals can be seen.

May
It is spring. It is warmer. Plants are growing taller and stronger; vegetables and fruits start to grow.

June
It is summer. The longest day is around 21 June. It is getting hotter. We water plants as there is less rain. We wear sun hats. Fruits and vegetables grow. Scandinavian people celebrate Midsummer.

July
It is summer. It is hotter. We need to water our plants as there is less rain. It is sunny and sometimes cloudy. Lots of insects.

August
It is summer. It is hotter. We need to water our plants as there is less rain. It is sunny and sometimes cloudy. Lots of insects.

Priming: memory cues to aid remembering

Priming

'The activation of certain thoughts or feelings that make them easier to think of and act upon' (Kearns & Lee, 2015)

Prime	Question	Think hard	Framework to respond

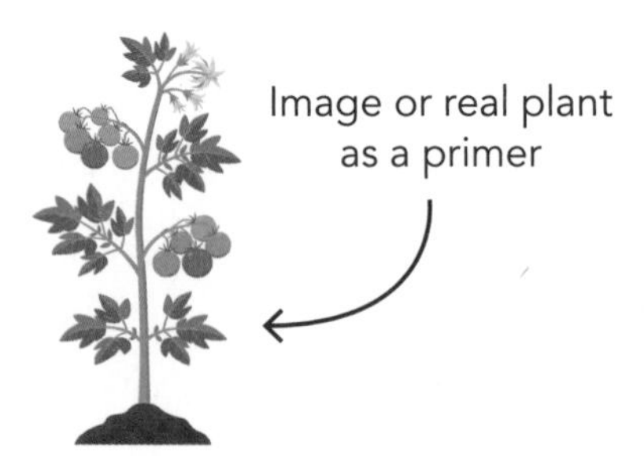		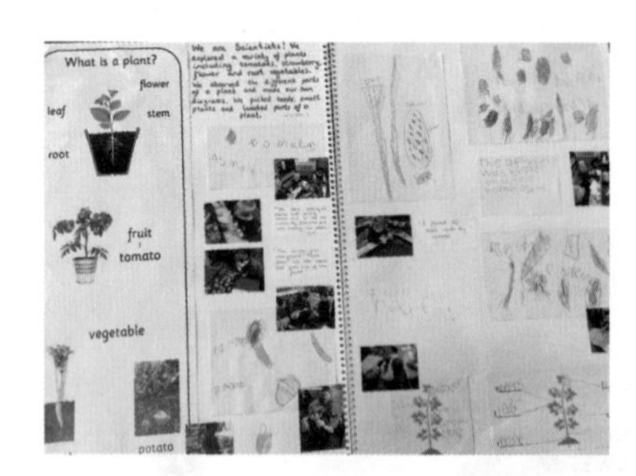	
'I'm going to ask you some questions about plants.'	*'Here's my question. Let's say it together...'* | *'What is a plant?'*	Rehearse and retrieve using known vocabulary from prior learning. Refer to and use their floor book as a simple, physical cue.	*'So, tell me, what is a plant?'* Structured conversations focus attention on the intended learning, including giant EYFS knowledge notes.

How the Great Teaching Toolkit and EYFS: Language of Learning align

Evidence Based Education's Great Teaching Toolkit
(Coe et al, 2020)

EYFS: Language of Learning

Understand the content

What foundational knowledge do children need to know?

What language opportunities do your children need more of?

- Teachers and practitioners use the language development framework as well as the supporting materials to focus on impactful research and physical development opportunities, provision and experiences.

Create a supportive environment

How well does the provision engage children in rich and structured language opportunities?

How are stories and books used to build strong relationships, focus attention and sustain interest?

- Increased opportunity for positive and cooperative sustained shared thinking and structured conversations.
- Through shared dialogue, and a love of books and stories, a culture of trust, high expectations and challenge is created.

Maximise the opportunity to learn

How well are routines modelled and embedded in daily practice?

What deliberate choices are made to build precise physical development routines into daily practice, targeting the vestibular system, proprioception and interoception?

- A language-rich provision that enables teacher and pupils to interact and acquire or sophisticate the foundational language needed to thrive.
- Focus on learner motivation and attention through knowing more about physical development.
- Distractions are reduced to maximise the opportunity for children to attend to and sustain learning.

Activate pupils' thinking

Is learning the key focus when planning activities for children?

Do children think hard during activities? How well do adults intervene with insightful questions, at the right time?

- A structured language development framework to help settings provide content, activities and interactions that activate children to think hard.

Ask yourself...

If you were asked these questions, how would you answer?

1. How does your setting provide opportunities, provision and experiences that are guided by cognitive science and neuroscience?
2. How are spaced retrieval practice and retrieval practice enacted in your setting?
3. How does provision planning support spaced retrieval practice and priming?
4. How does your enabling environment support pupils to develop their executive function skills?
5. How do you enable pupils to attend to the desired learning?
6. How do you know your pupils are acquiring, using and remembering the foundational knowledge they need to build coherent long-term memory?

Chapter 4

Why physical development and sensory integration matter

The vestibular system, proprioception and interoception

Physical development questions every setting should ask

Extracted from the Department for Education's *Statutory Framework for the Early Years Foundation Stage* (2023)

Reasons why physical development is a prime area of learning

We need to pay attention to pupil's physical development, now more than ever.

With many of our pupils leading more sedentary lifestyles (linked to increased use of technology and screens, and other factors such as a lack of physical space) and the lingering effects of the Covid-19 pandemic impacting the youngest pupils in our care, we cannot assume that pupils will enter our settings with age-appropriate physical development. Under-developed physical competence can have a profound impact upon other aspects of learning.

The pandemic also contributed to the under-development of some children's vestibular sense and proprioception. Many settings are encountering this in the form of perceived learning difficulties where attention, physical competence and coordination systems are under-developed. It is key to ensure that children have targeted, repeated and frequent experience to help mature these senses.

Why pay attention to physical development?

- The development of movement skills influences attention, cognition, thinking skills and memory.
- Physical development brings a child into contact with new challenges that affirm or test their self-confidence/self-belief.
- Supporting young children's physical development supports their overall achievement.

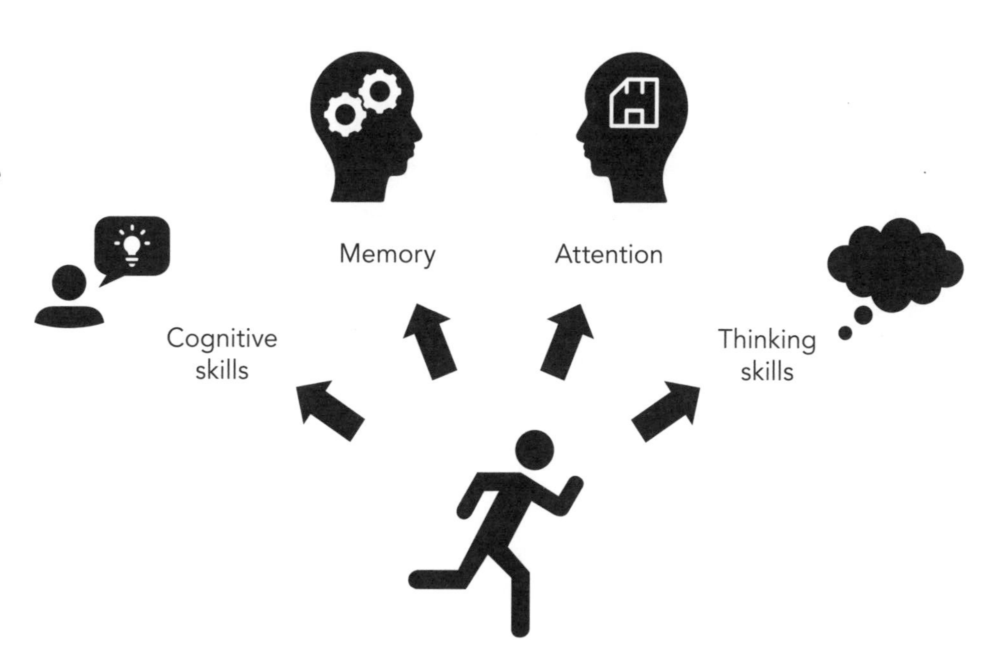

Reasons why physical development is a prime area of learning

The eight senses and physical development

Most of us are familiar with the traditional five senses: sight, smell, taste, hearing and touch. The three lesser-known senses refer to our **movement and balance** (vestibular), our **body position** (proprioception) and **internal signals** (interoception). These are essential to physical development.

Sight or vision

Smell or olfaction

Taste or gustation

Hearing or audition

Touch or somatosensory

Vestibular system

Proprioception

Interoception

In order to pay attention to physical development, we need to look at what the research tells us about how sensory development enables us to learn.

The learning pyramid, devised by the occupational therapists Mary Sue Williams and Sherry Shellenberger (1996), proposes that learning is incremental and that a child's **sensory integration** plays a huge part in their development.

The learning pyramid demonstrates the way in which our bodies 'organise' input from the world in which we live. If any aspect of sensory integration is under-developed, this can impact on other aspects of development and, in particular, on the development of the prime areas.

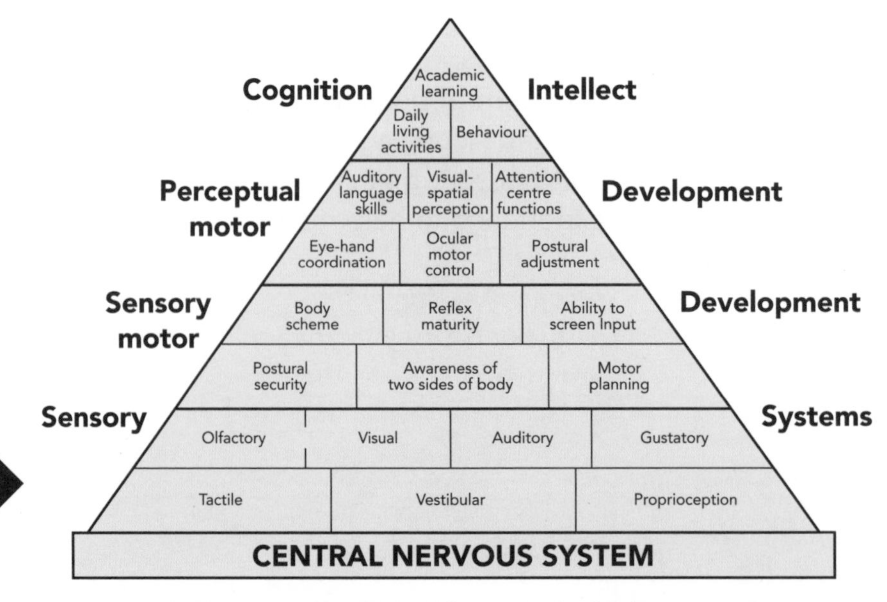

The learning pyramid, Williams & Shellenberger, 1996

What is the vestibular sense?

Essentially, our vestibular sense helps us to understand the position and motion of the head, which in turn helps us to determine whether we are moving or still, upright or upside down.

The vestibular sense is fundamental to the development of balance and helps us to understand our relationship to gravity. Situated in the inner ear, it is the most connected sensory system in our body. It works alongside our other sensory systems (including the proprioceptive sense), enabling us to use our eyes effectively and to process sounds in our environment, as well as language.

Our vestibular sense has a profound impact on our physical, emotional and learning development. It is the first sensory system to develop in the womb. When a foetus is only five months old, its vestibular system is very well developed. The vestibular sense provides the growing foetal brain with a wide range of sensory information, as the foetus is rocked back and forth by its mother's movements.

After birth, our vestibular system is often likened to a traffic controller for the brain, for all the sensory information it receives. It sorts and relays incoming sensory information from other sensory organs, and passes this information on to the various sensory regions of the brain.

The vestibular system is a traffic controller for the brain

The vestibular sense is the brain's traffic controller; it sorts and relays information from other sensory organs and passes it on to various sensory regions of the brain. It is crucial for child development and affects physical, emotional and learning skills.

The vestibular system is located in our inner ear. It supports balance – for example, as a child wobbles on one leg to get dressed, the vestibular system detects their head movements, sending signals to the brain, which in turn sends signals to the body, telling it how to respond and stay balanced.

- The vestibular system helps us to keep tabs on the position and motion of the head and enables effective use of our eyes. It allows us to process environmental sounds.
- It supports confidence and safety during movement activities, and helps to coordinate both sides of the body.
- It is connected and works alongside our other sensory systems (including proprioception).
- The vestibular sense affects language development, as it integrates with auditory and visual senses.

How to support and improve the vestibular sense

Swinging.

Using a rocking chair.

Using playground equipment – roundabout, spinning cups, seesaws, slides.

Bouncing on a mini trampoline.

Bouncing on a therapy ball (prone, supine, sitting).

Using space hoppers.

Rolling around and down.

Riding bikes, trikes, scooters and scooter boards.

Walking on uneven surfaces or a 'tight rope' (a chalk line or skipping rope on the floor); playing Twister or hopscotch.

Yoga poses such as downward dog, plank, airplane, tree, dancer, warrior one.

What you need to know...

What you need to know about me if my vestibular sense is not working as it should

- My learning and behaviour may be affected, and others may think I am 'hyper' or 'slow'.
- I may appear clumsy.
- It is a lot easier for me to balance when moving than when standing still.
- I may manage the problem of my 'sleepy' vestibular system by tending to daydream, or, conversely, I may want to move and fidget as this stimulates my vestibular system.
- If you give me too much information, I may avoid things – e.g. sports.
- I may get nauseous when in a car/travelling.
- I may have delayed or poor language.
- My sleepy vestibular system can keep my cortex worrying about staying upright and balanced, leaving no time for it to perform its other jobs (memory, thinking, learning, reasoning, problem-solving, emotions, consciousness, attention).

I may find it difficult to...

- Smoothly look up at a whiteboard, then down at my work.
- Sit still! I may bounce/spin/rock/move constantly.
- Keep my eyes still so images aren't bouncing all over the place.
- Read effortlessly (as I find it hard to scan a line of text).
- Enjoy sports – keeping track of a moving ball may be tricky.
- Hold myself up properly – I may lie on the floor instead of sitting up on the carpet, or lean on my elbow when at a desk (poor posture).
- Focus/attend to learning.
- Coordinate myself or balance.
- Speak clearly.

What is proprioception?

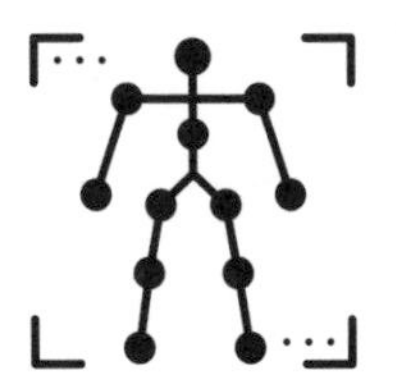

In simple terms, proprioception is the sense that informs the body about its position in space. It plays a large role in self-regulation, coordination, posture, body awareness, speech and the ability to focus. Proprioception allows us to perceive the location of our body parts, their movements and the required muscle strength.

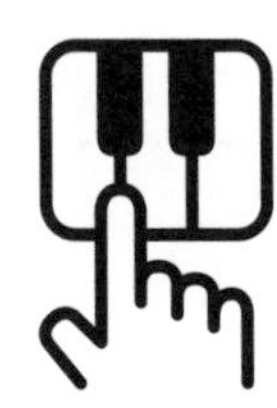

Sensory receptors in the skin, muscles and joints provide us with proprioceptive input. Activities like playing the piano, handwriting and sports require substantial proprioceptive input.

When specialised receptors called proprioceptors are stimulated, they relay information about our movements and body posture to the brain's arousal centre. Within this system, three key components of the brain (the cortex, the limbic system and the cerebellum) interact and influence a child's level of alertness.

By incorporating proprioceptive input into children's daily routines, we can support them in maintaining an optimal state for learning and focused attention.

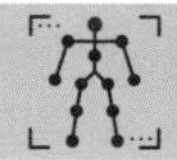 Proprioceptive receptors are deep within our joints and muscles

Proprioception is crucial for child development because it impacts on physical, emotional and learning skills. The proprioceptive sense is stimulated every time we move and creates a map in our mind of where our body parts are. Proprioception is in use each time we use our muscles, stretch or bend our joints. Whenever we push, pull or lift heavy things, we really stimulate this sense – it helps us to know how much force to use.

Proprioception tells us where our body parts are and what they are doing. For example, if we have an itch, this sense tells us where to scratch without needing to look. It aids our spatial awareness and helps us to know how our body fits into the surrounding environment. Linked to motor planning, proprioception supports the coordination between our body parts and senses, including the parts of the body we need for speech.

How to support and improve proprioception

Pushing, pulling and heavy muscle work.

Stretching, jumping, running, climbing, hanging, stomping, bouncing.

Wheelbarrow walking, crab walking, pushing a scooter board.

Kicking a ball or against a resistance band, jumping jacks.

Crawling.

Chewing, drinking through a straw.

Squeezing, stretching and pulling on resistance bands.

Yoga poses such as downward dog, plank, airplane, tree, dancer, warrior one.

What you need to know...

What you need to know about me if my proprioceptive sense is not working as it should

- It can affect my learning and behaviour, and others' responses to me.
- I may have difficulty knowing where my body is in space and understanding boundaries when playing and interacting with other children.
- I may like rough-and-tumble play; I may be rough with my peers (biting/pushing/kicking).
- I may deliberately bump and crash into things.
- I may bang things against other objects.
- I might tap my foot a lot – I need to check where it is.
- I might rock in my chair as I need to know that I'm not going to fall off.
- I might drop things frequently.
- I might press too hard with my pencil or not know how to hold delicate things.
- I might fall over a lot/may appear clumsy.
- I may not be able to get all my words out (I may get frustrated with this!).

I may find it difficult to...

- Focus/attend to learning.
- Sit still.
- Know how much pressure I need to apply when holding things or using tools.
- Relate to others' needs.
- Coordinate my body.
- Multi-task/do more than one thing at a time.
- Keep myself safe.
- Motor plan (standing on one foot/navigating stairs or steps).
- Speak clearly (this is linked to my motor planning).
- Hold myself up properly – I may slump instead of sitting upright, or lean on my elbow when at a desk/put my head on the desk (poor posture).

What is interoception?

The interoceptive system senses internal signals from your body that tell it when you are hungry, when you need the toilet, when your heart is beating fast, when you feel hot or cold, or when you are in pain.

Children who find it hard to sense their internal signals often struggle to work out which emotion they are feeling and may have difficulty recognising emotions in other people. In contrast, children who find it easy to sense internal signals may experience their emotions more intensely. This can affect self-regulation and how they respond to others.

Just like our other senses, interoception is important for our survival, emotions, decisions and wellbeing. Although it is important to ask, 'How are you feeling?', it is just as important to ask, '**What** are you feeling?'

How to support and improve interoception

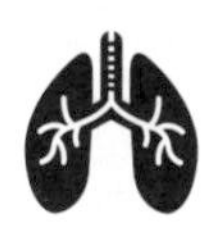

Breathing exercises.

Yoga poses such as downward dog, plank, airplane, tree, dancer, warrior one.

Alerting activities such as feeling hot and cold things and noticing the difference, feeling your heartbeat, and noticing breathing through exercise/getting out of breath.

Activities that involve the large muscles in your body, e.g. pushing, pulling, (large) digging, sweeping.

Recommended resources to support the vestibular sense and proprioception

We recommend brilliant resources to support systematic and essential programmes that will enhance EYFS provision. The Whole of Me (www.thewholeofme.com) is a comprehensive toolkit for teachers to bring stories to life using yoga-inspired moves and songs. The toolkit is based around eight key themes of wellbeing and learning attitudes. It offers extension materials to create new stories, understand the moves and their benefits, and branch into other areas of the curriculum.

Why move?

The movements linked to each story stretch and move the whole of the body, not just specific muscle groups. The yoga-inspired moves develop postural control and coordination, including fine motor skills and crossing the midline, both of which are critical for developing writing and learning skills. Additionally, following simple sequences within the stories helps children to learn routines and develop key academic skills like comprehension, memory and enquiry.

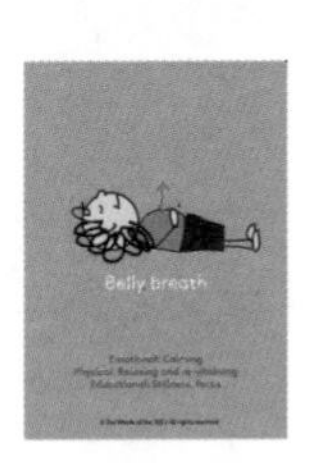

Relax...

At the end of each story is a relaxation song and posture focusing on stillness and reflection. The relaxation songs used in The Whole of Me can be used on their own at any time when you want to create a sense of calmness among pupils. Other postures such as mountain, feather and butterfly also help to create calm and focus. You can create stories about calmness and discuss how they make the children feel.

Support

The Whole of Me offers easy-to-follow instructional videos for every posture. As you go through each theme, you will build a valuable repertoire of moves that can be brought into your own unique story sessions. You can encourage pupils to put together two or three moves that they enjoy in order to tell their own stories. There are endless possibilities for creativity and exploration.

CAT AND THE WONDER OF SNOW

What you need: DRUM (BELL & SHAKER for transitions)

Cat was slowly waking up. She looked out from under her paw and noticed that it was snowing.

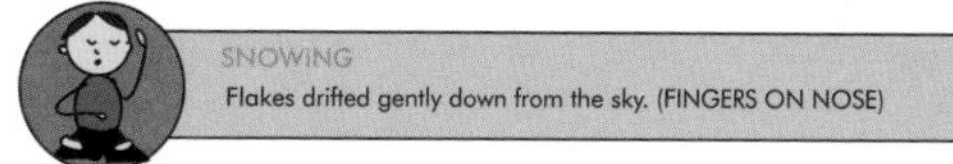

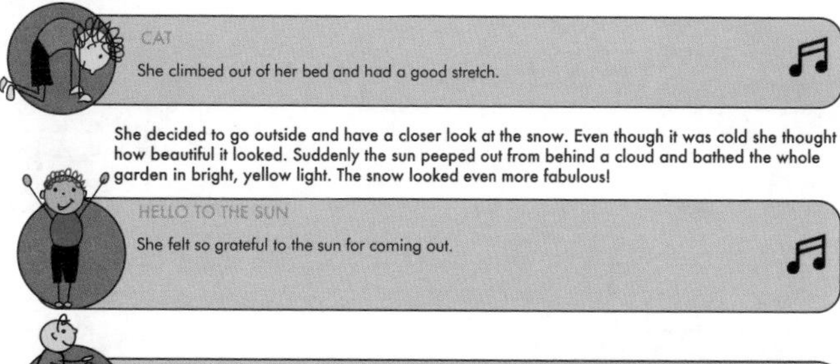

WALKING

She continued to walk across the sun and noticed the wonderful crunching sound it made.

Cat looked over the fence and noticed a dog who looked quite sad.

DOG

'Are you alright Dog?' Dog looked up, ' It's so cold, all I can think of is how cold I am!'

Cat replied, ' If you take a minute to notice how beautiful everything looks in the snow you won't feel the cold as much.'

BREATH

Dog did as Cat suggested and noticed the snow. He heard the crunching sound it made. He was grateful for the light of the sun.' (3 BREATHS)

'Thank you Cat,' woofed Dog. 'You're right! There is so much to be thankful for.'

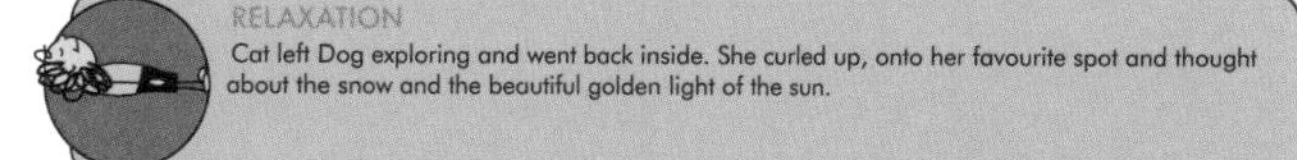

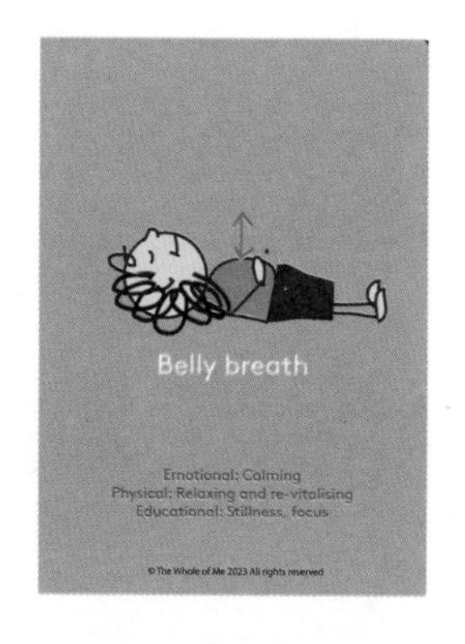

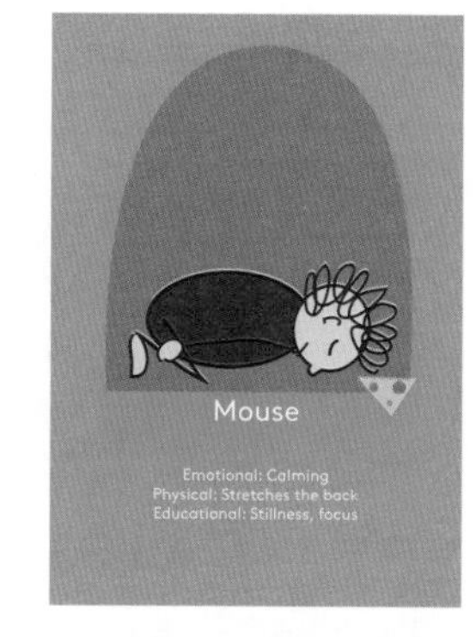

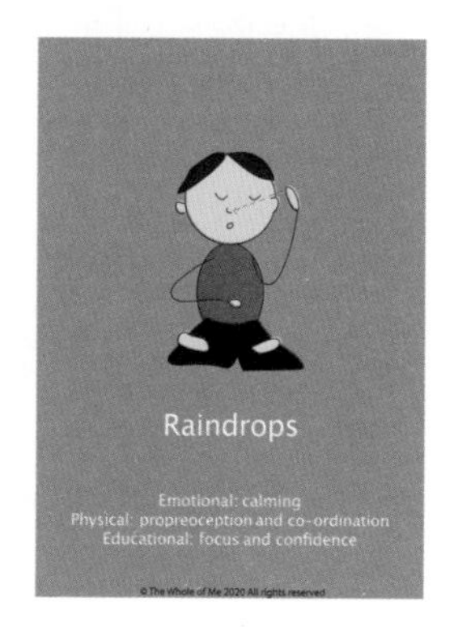

Practice to support the vestibular sense and proprioception

EYFS: deliberate physical development – story, music, posture control and orientation

Alex uses an iPad with screen mirroring and Keynote to focus attention, give clear explanations and examples, and engage children in attempting and applying self-regulation.

The story is the golden thread that connects the children and supports their attention and participation.

CUSP lesson routines (born from CUSP Reading) are infused throughout all areas of learning and subjects. Here, Alex models how…

1

The story setting is described and images shown of a beautiful pond with lily flowers. The focus is on listening to the bees.

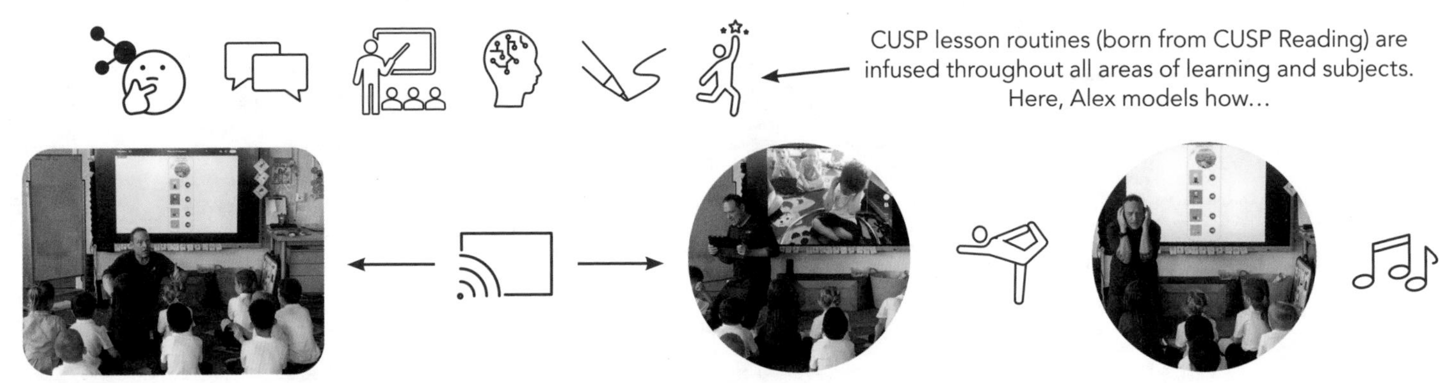

Alex designed the resources into an interactive knowledge note using Keynote. This interactive knowledge note is a simple, physical point of reference – it has all the images and music embedded. It is screen-mirrored to the TV from the iPad.

Children copy the explanation and examples. They also model to the class in the sharing station (which is actually a hoop).

Attempt and apply – the class practise the physical development position with music that is played directly from the iPad, with sound through the TV screen.

2

The frog who couldn't sit still is introduced. The children become physically active through structured movement.

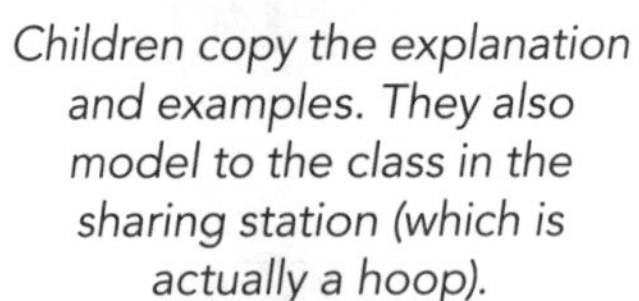

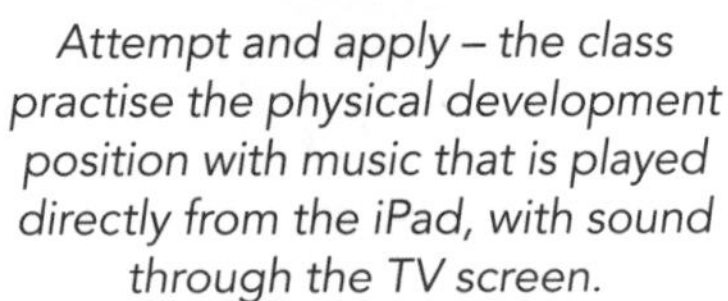

Language development is carefully woven in to support children with self-regulation.

Physical movement and positions are precise and deliberate. It is clear to see where additional opportunities can be planned for children who present less attention, balance and coordination. This is fed forward into provision and activities.

In partnership with the brilliant Houldsworth Valley Primary Academy – thank you, Sophie, for lending me your Reception class every week.

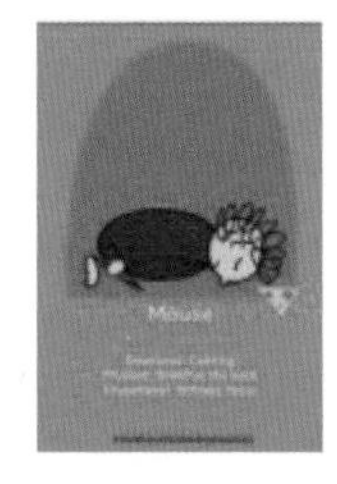

To help the frog self-regulate, we have to try to help it be as still as a mouse – posture, position and calming music.

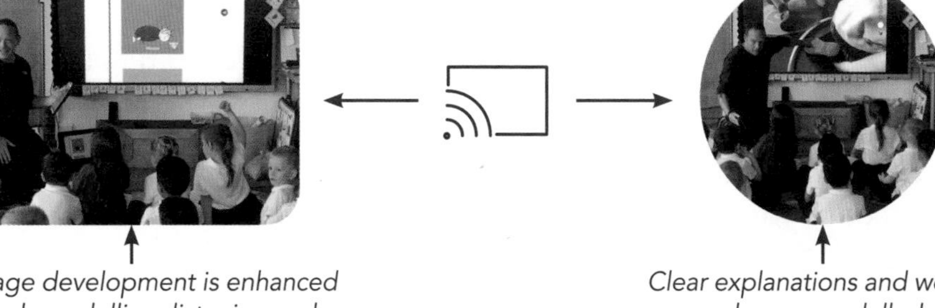

Language development is enhanced through modelling, listening and questioning using the EYFS: Language of Learning development framework.

Clear explanations and worked examples are modelled using screen-sharing. This offers precision and accuracy.

Attempt and apply – children practise the position and breathing using a concrete mental model as their focus.

To further help the frog calm and be still, we show how to belly-breathe using bean bags or quoits. Music helps self-regulation.

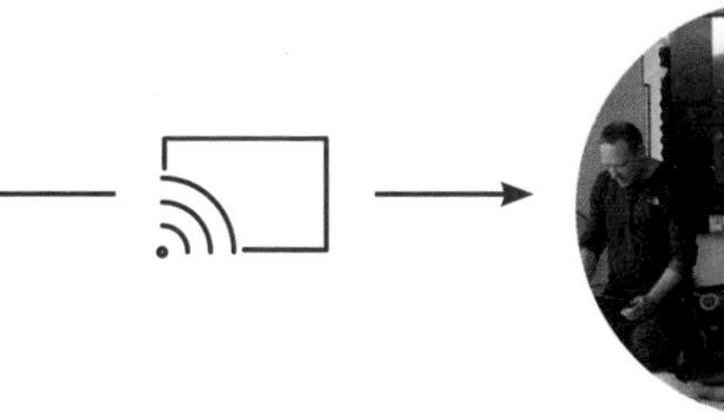

Challenge

The story sequence is combined and retold with image cues, language position, movement and response to music, as children practise self-regulation.

 +  +  + 

This is cumulative and highly repeatable, so children become a little more expert as the routine becomes embedded.

Ask yourself...

If you were asked these questions, how would you answer?

1. How well does your setting utilise the most current research around physical and sensory development to meet the needs of pupils with attention, balance and coordination difficulties?

2. What professional development do staff need to bring about strategic and cumulative opportunities, provision and experiences to meet the needs of pupils who find it hard to concentrate, stick at a task, manage their body position and emotions, or coordinate their actions?

3. What opportunities, provision and experiences does your setting deliberately choose, over time, to focus attention and help children make sense of the intended learning?

4. How does your setting prioritise physical and sensory development, with a focus on improving attention, balance and coordination?

5. How well do all staff know each and every child's physical development, balance, coordination and attention needs, and how do you ensure that children who are behind their expected developmental milestones are able to catch up?

Chapter 5

Worked examples of using the language development framework

Worked examples

Physical development

Sensory and gross motor

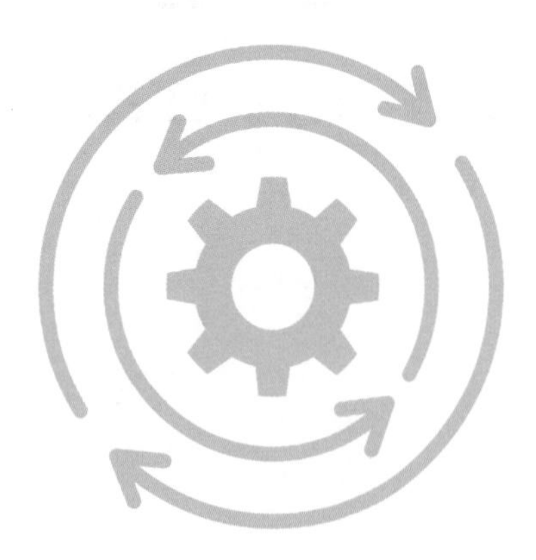

Maya's Walk by Moira Butterfield and Kim Geyer

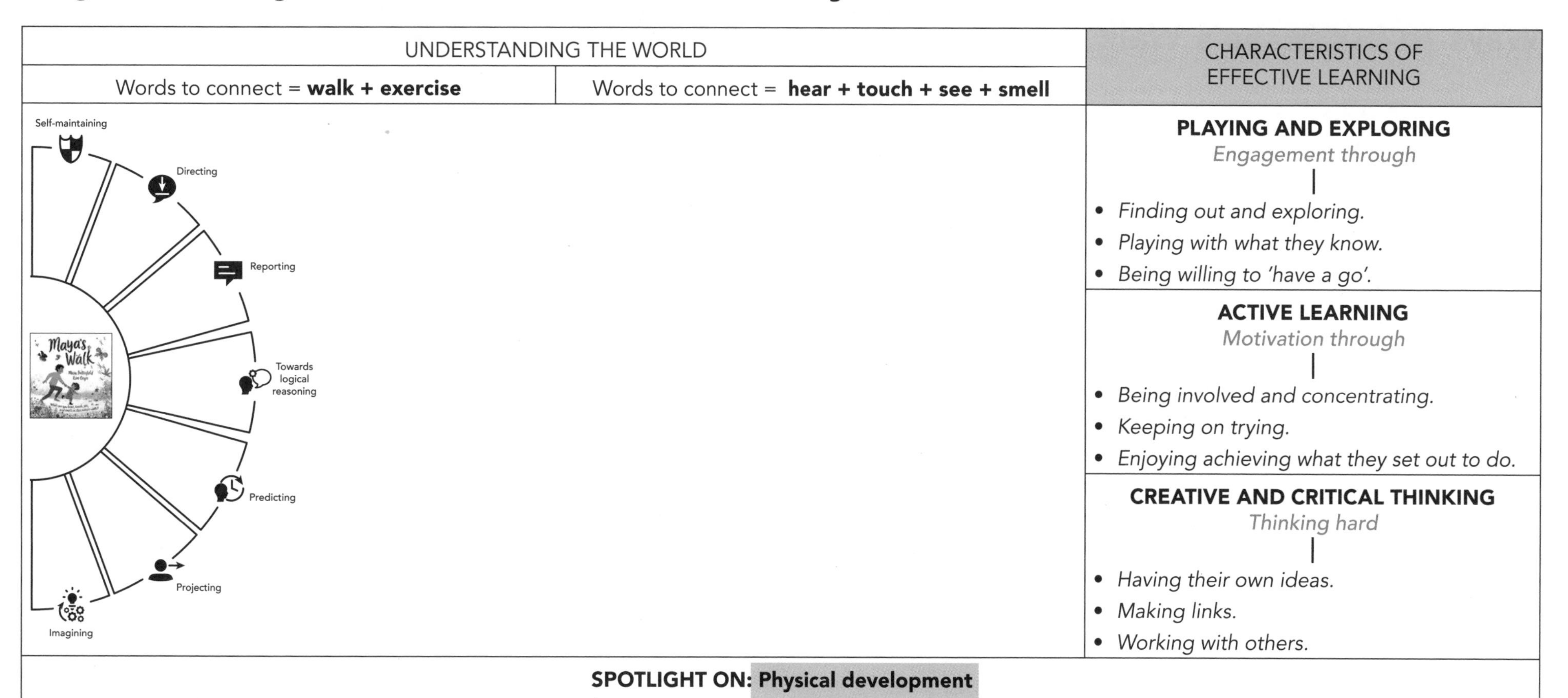

UNDERSTANDING THE WORLD		CHARACTERISTICS OF EFFECTIVE LEARNING
Words to connect = **walk + exercise**	Words to connect = **hear + touch + see + smell**	

PLAYING AND EXPLORING

Engagement through

- *Finding out and exploring.*
- *Playing with what they know.*
- *Being willing to 'have a go'.*

ACTIVE LEARNING

Motivation through

- *Being involved and concentrating.*
- *Keeping on trying.*
- *Enjoying achieving what they set out to do.*

CREATIVE AND CRITICAL THINKING

Thinking hard

- *Having their own ideas.*
- *Making links.*
- *Working with others.*

SPOTLIGHT ON: Physical development

ELG: Gross motor skills (DfE, 2023)

'Children at the expected level of development will:

- Negotiate space and obstacles safely, with consideration for themselves and others.
- Demonstrate strength, balance and coordination when playing.
- Move energetically, such as running, jumping, dancing, hopping, skipping and climbing.'

National curriculum: KS1 physical education (DfE, 2013)

'Pupils should be taught to:

- Master basic movements including running, jumping, throwing and catching, as well as developing balance, agility and co-ordination, and begin to apply these in a range of activities.
- Participate in team games, developing simple tactics for attacking and defending.
- Perform dances using simple movement patterns.'

Ways to use Maya's Walk

Maya's Walk by Moira Butterfield and Kim Geyer is a beautiful book that presents children with concrete examples of a great variety of movement, pathways and levels. We can also draw sensory experiences from this book that can be easily planned into the provision in our settings.

The types of questions we ask children at the point of provision and during an activity can add incredible richness to their language. It is important to time the questions thoughtfully, without unnecessarily interrupting focus and learning.

An essential part of asking a question is to **listen** to the response and build forward with rich dialogue. We are not testing children on what they know; we are asking questions in order to listen to their explanations and use of language. From there, we can work out what pupils need to consolidate or what they need in order to elaborate their language. This can be done be in collaboration with children.

- How well do they **explain and model** what they know and can do (reporting)? Can they show and monitor through language the different ways of moving that they have experienced?
- Do they begin to **reason and make sense** of the learning? How do they know (reasoning)? Can they explain why they are moving in such a way and some of the things they did to overcome any difficulties they faced?
- Can they **predict and plan** to use what they know (predicting)? Are they able to think ahead and foresee what could happen in a known scenario or prior experience?
- How well do they explain and show their understanding of empathy and the feelings of others (projecting)?
- Can they build on prior physical experiences and imagine alternative and fantastical ways of enacting them (imagining)?

Questions to check for language development and understanding

 Reporting	 Towards logical reasoning	 Predicting	 Projecting	 Imagining
Identify the components of the images or book | *'What do you see on this page?'* *'Who is on this page?'* *'Describe the page with the birds singing – how are people moving on this page?'* **Refer to detail: the colour and shape, size or position of an object** | *'What movements are they doing on the animal page? What shapes are they making?'* **Elaboration** **Identify and describe images or scenes from the book** | *'Tell me, what is happening here [on page where they are jumping]?'* **Talk about a sequence of events** | *'What happened in the story? What did Maya and her dad hear, touch, see and smell on their walk?'* *'Tell me about how they exercised.'*	**Explain a process** | *'What different types of exercise did they do? Can you show me?'* **Recognise problems and causes** | *'What problem did the man with the dog have? Why?'* *'Was the rain a problem? Why?'* *'What problem might the boy/girl with the paper boats have? What about the boy with the kite?'* *'Why shouldn't the little boy get too close to the pond?'* **Recognise casual and dependent relationships** | *'Why are Maya's walks important?'* *'What senses did she use on her walk and why?'* **Justify judgements and actions** | *'Why did Maya and her dad go for a walk?'*	**Anticipate or forecast** | *'Which walk do you think Maya will choose next? Why?'* **Predict the consequences of actions and events** | *'Tell me, why is exercise important?'* *'What else could Maya and her dad have felt on the walk?'* **Survey for possible alternatives** | *'If it were raining all the way through, how would that change the walk?'*	**Project into the experiences, feelings and reactions of others** | *'How do you think Maya's dad felt on the walk?'* *'How do you think Maya felt when it rained?'* *'What do you think Maya will dream of?'* **Reflect on the meaning of experiences** | *'How did you feel when you saw the rainbow?'* *'How do you feel when you exercise?'* **Project into a situation never experienced** | *'If you were on a walk with Maya and her dad, which animals would you have copied?'* *'How do you think it felt on the boat?'*	**In an imagined context** | Using puppets, characters or a phone or walkie-talkie.    *'Pretend to be Maya saying all the things she did on her walk.'* *'Can we be Maya walking? What might she be saying as she goes?'* *'Pretend to be Maya hop-hop-hopping, dancing, prancing down the path, singing, clapping to the beat. What shall we sing?'* *'Can we copy the animals? Let's be creeping cats. What noise do cats make?'* This is a good opportunity to observe pupil movement.

Worked examples

Personal social emotional development

Building relationships

The Way Back Home by Oliver Jeffers

UNDERSTANDING THE WORLD		CHARACTERISTICS OF EFFECTIVE LEARNING
Words to connect = **dark + night**	Words to connect = **travel + space**	

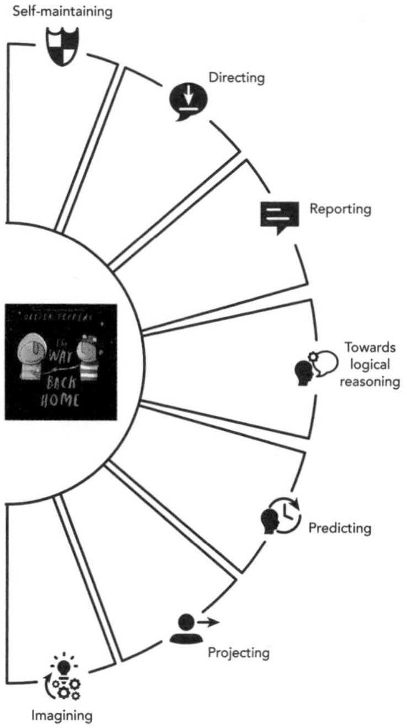

Self-maintaining

Directing

Reporting

Towards logical reasoning

Predicting

Projecting

Imagining

PLAYING AND EXPLORING

Engagement through

- *Finding out and exploring.*
- *Playing with what they know.*
- *Being willing to 'have a go'.*

ACTIVE LEARNING

Motivation through

- *Being involved and concentrating.*
- *Keeping on trying.*
- *Enjoying achieving what they set out to do.*

CREATIVE AND CRITICAL THINKING

Thinking hard

- *Having their own ideas.*
- *Making links.*
- *Working with others.*

SPOTLIGHT ON: Personal, social and emotional development

ELG: Building relationships (DfE, 2023)

'Children at the expected level of development will:

- Work and play cooperatively and take turns with others.
- Form positive attachments to adults and friendships with peers.
- Show sensitivity to their own and to others' needs.'

KS1/2 relationships education (DfE, 2019)

'By the end of primary school, pupils should know:

- The characteristics of friendships, including mutual respect, truthfulness, trustworthiness, loyalty, kindness, generosity, trust, sharing interests and experiences and support with problems and difficulties.
- That healthy friendships are positive and welcoming towards others, and do not make others feel lonely or excluded.
- That most friendships have ups and downs, and that these can often be worked through so that the friendship is repaired or even strengthened, and that resorting to violence is never right.'

Questions to check for language development and understanding

 Reporting	 Towards logical reasoning	 Predicting	Projecting	Imagining
Talk about a sequence of events | *'I've got four images from the story here – put them in order.'* **Refer to detail: the colour and shape, size or position of an object/character** | *'Describe what the Moon/ aeroplane looks like.'* *'What does the Martian look like?'* **Elaboration** **Identify and describe images or scenes from the book** | *'Tell me, what is happening here?'* *'Who is this? What is the boy doing?'* **Absence of conditions** | *'Why did the plane start to splutter?'* *'Why did the Martian's spacecraft land with a bump on the Moon?'* **Reflect on the meaning of experiences** | *'What **trouble** did the boy and the Martian find themselves in?'*	**Explain a process** | *'What did the boy and the Martian do to help each other?'* *'How did the boy and the Martian solve problems with their engines?'* **Recognise casual and dependent relationships** | *'How come the boy and the Martian both ended up on the Moon?'* *'What did the boy and the Martian first think of each other? Why do you think that?'* **Recognise problems and causes** | *'What problem did the boy and the Martian share?'* **Justify judgements and actions** | *'Was it a good idea for the boy to jump down from the Moon to get things to mend their engines?'* *'How do the words **alone** and **afraid** tell us how the boy and the Martian felt?'*	**Anticipate or forecast** | *'Tell me, what happened when the two stranded travellers landed on the Moon?'* *'What did the Martian think when the boy left to get tools and petrol?'* **Survey for possible alternatives** | *'Could the boy and the Martian have solved the problem in any other way?'* **Predict the consequences of actions and events** | *'If the boy was stranded alone on the Moon, what could have happened?'* **Recognise problems and solutions** | *'If the boy stayed at home watching his favourite programme, what could the problem be for the Martian?'*	**Project into the experiences, feelings and reactions of others** | *'Before their eyes became used to the dark, why might the boy and the Martian have feared the worst?'* *'What if the boy had not returned to the Moon? How would he have felt?'* **Project into a situation never experienced** | *'If you were the boy, alone on the Moon, how do you think you might feel? Why?'* *'Imagine the Martian wasn't friendly. What could have happened?'*	**In an imagined context** | Using puppets, characters or a phone or walkie-talkie.    *'Hello, little boy. What is wrong with your plane? How do you know?'* *'Hello, Martian. What is wrong with your spacecraft? How do you know?'* *'Hello, Martian. What does your space craft need to make it work? Why is that?'* *'Hello, little boy. What does your plane need? Why is that?'* *'Pretend to be the boy – describe your world to the Martian.'* *'I can see…'* *'Pretend to be the Martian – describe your world to the boy.'* *'I can see…'*

Worked examples

Literacy

Comprehension

Three Billy Goats Gruff by Alison Edgson

LITERACY AND UNDERSTANDING THE WORLD		CHARACTERISTICS OF EFFECTIVE LEARNING
Words to connect = **goat + bridge + troll**	Words to connect = **feelings + brave**	

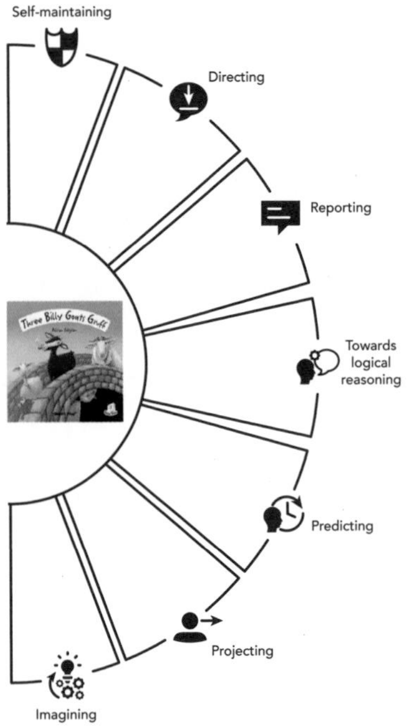

Self-maintaining
Directing
Reporting
Towards logical reasoning
Predicting
Projecting
Imagining

PLAYING AND EXPLORING
Engagement through

- *Finding out and exploring.*
- *Playing with what they know.*
- *Being willing to 'have a go'.*

ACTIVE LEARNING
Motivation through

- *Being involved and concentrating.*
- *Keeping on trying.*
- *Enjoying achieving what they set out to do.*

CREATIVE AND CRITICAL THINKING
Thinking hard

- *Having their own ideas.*
- *Making links.*
- *Working with others.*

SPOTLIGHT ON: Literacy – comprehension

ELG: Comprehension (DfE, 2023)

'Children at the expected level of development will:

- Demonstrate understanding of what has been read to them by retelling stories and narratives using their own words and recently introduced vocabulary.
- Anticipate – where appropriate – key events in stories.
- Use and understand recently introduced vocabulary during discussions about stories, non-fiction, rhymes and poems and during role-play.'

National curriculum: Year 1 reading comprehension (DfE, 2013)

'Pupils should be taught to develop pleasure in reading, motivation to read, vocabulary and understanding by:

- Listening to and discussing a wide range of poems, stories and non-fiction at a level beyond that at which they can read independently.
- Being encouraged to link what they read or hear read to their own experiences.
- Becoming very familiar with key stories, fairy stories and traditional tales, retelling them and considering their particular characteristics.
- Recognising and joining in with predictable phrases.
- Learning to appreciate rhymes and poems, and to recite some by heart.
- Discussing word meanings, linking new meanings to those already known.

Understand both the books they can already read accurately and fluently and those they listen to by:

- Drawing on what they already know or on background. Information and vocabulary provided by the teacher.
- Checking that the text makes sense to them as they read and correcting inaccurate reading.
- Discussing the significance of the title and events.
- Making inferences on the basis of what is being said and done
- Predicting what might happen on the basis of what has been read so far.

Participate in discussion about what is read to them, taking turns and listening to what others say.
Explain clearly their understanding of what is read to them.'

Questions to check for language development and understanding

 Reporting	Towards logical reasoning	Predicting	Projecting	Imagining
Elaboration **Identify and describe images or scenes from the book** *'Tell me, what happens when something crosses the bridge?* *'Who is this in this picture? What is the troll doing?'* **Refer to detail: the colour and shape, size or position of an object/character** *'What does the small billy goat look like?'* *'Describe the troll to me.'* **Talk about a sequence of events** *'What did the troll do after the first billy goat crossed the bridge?'* **Absence of conditions** *'What made the billy goats want to cross the bridge?'* **Reflect on the meaning of experiences** *'How did you feel when the little billy goat approached the bridge for the first time?'*	**Explain a process** *'How did the billy goats decide to get across the bridge?'* **Recognise casual and dependent relationships** *'What made the billy goats cross the bridge and risk being gobbled up by the troll?'* *'How did the smallest and middle-sized billy goats not get eaten by the troll?'* **Recognise problems and causes** *'Why was the troll a problem?'* **Justify judgements and actions** *'Was it a good idea for the little billy goat to cross the bridge first?'*	**Anticipate or forecast** *'Tell me, was the troll always going to lose? Why do you think that?'* **Survey for possible alternatives** *'Could the goats have solved the troll problem in another way?'* **Predict the consequences of actions and events** *'If the troll had tried to eat one of the goats, what do you think would have happened?'* **Recognition of problems and solutions** *'What if the grass wasn't so nice on the other side of the bridge? How would that change the story?'* *'Could the billy goats have helped the troll?'*	**Project into the experiences, feelings and reactions of others** *'Why did all the animals fear the troll? What tells you that in the story?'* *'What if the goats had never crossed the bridge? Would the story be the same?'* **Project into a situation never experienced** *'If you were a friendly troll, under the bridge, what would you have done?'* *'Imagine the troll was friendly – what would have happened then?'*	**In an imagined context** Using puppets, characters or a phone or walkie-talkie.    *'Hello, little billy goat. Why is the troll so grumpy? How do you know?'* *'Hello, troll. How could you help the goats instead of being grumpy?'* *'Hello, big billy goat. What does the troll need to be happier and more friendly?'* *'Pretend to be the troll – describe how you feel when you hear the little billy goat trip-trapping across the bridge.'* *'Pretend to be the little billy goat – describe what you saw when the troll poked his head up from beneath the bridge.'*

Worked examples

Mathematics

Number

Anno's Counting Book by Mitsumasa Anno

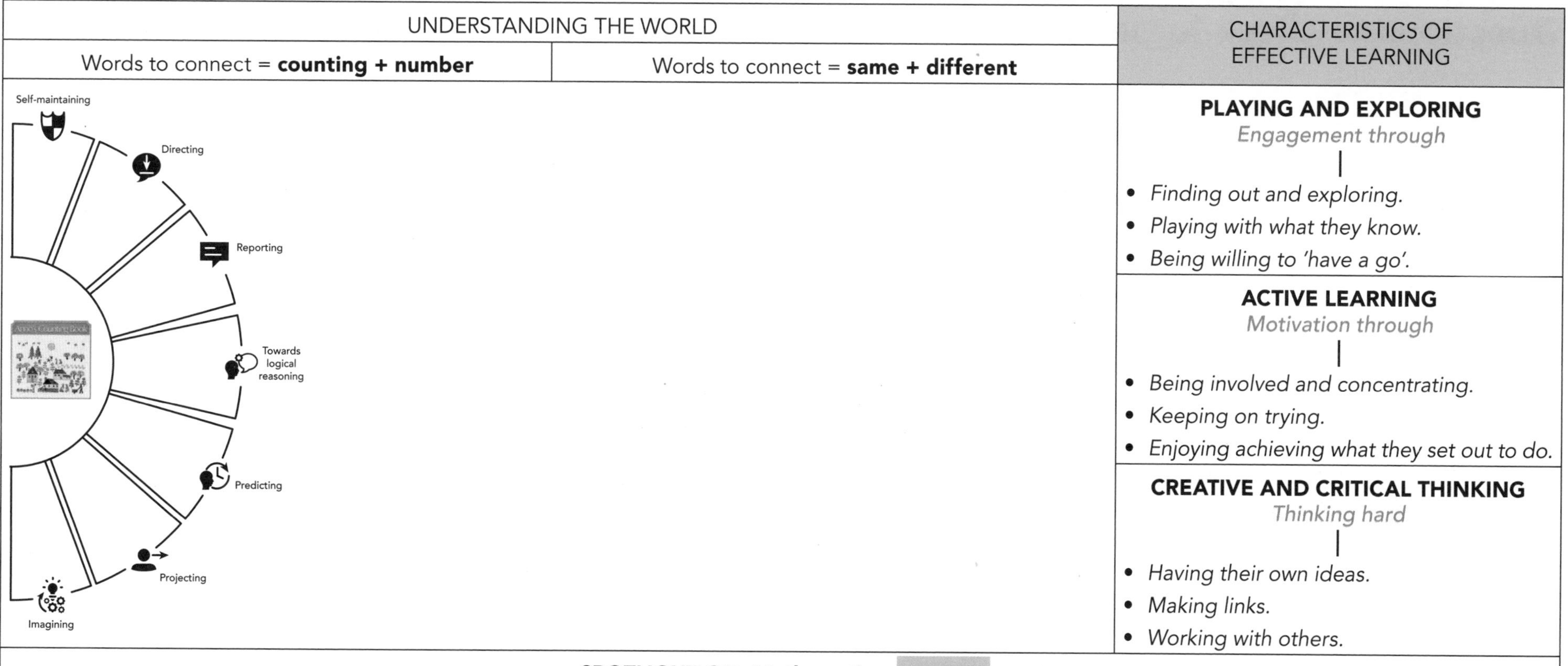

UNDERSTANDING THE WORLD		CHARACTERISTICS OF EFFECTIVE LEARNING
Words to connect = **counting + number**	Words to connect = **same + different**	
		PLAYING AND EXPLORING *Engagement through* • *Finding out and exploring.* • *Playing with what they know.* • *Being willing to 'have a go'.*
		ACTIVE LEARNING *Motivation through* • *Being involved and concentrating.* • *Keeping on trying.* • *Enjoying achieving what they set out to do.*
		CREATIVE AND CRITICAL THINKING *Thinking hard* • *Having their own ideas.* • *Making links.* • *Working with others.*

SPOTLIGHT ON: Mathematics – number

ELGs: Number and numerical patterns (DfE, 2023)

'Children at the expected level of development will:

- Have a deep understanding of number to 10, including the composition of each number.
- Subitise (recognise quantities without counting) up to 5.
- Automatically recall (without reference to rhymes, counting or other aids) number bonds up to 5 (including subtraction facts) and some number bonds to 10, including double facts.
- Verbally count beyond 20, recognising the pattern of the counting system.
- Compare quantities up to 10 in different contexts, recognising when one quantity is greater than, less than or the same as the other quantity.
- Explore and represent patterns within numbers up to 10, including evens and odds, double facts and how quantities can be distributed equally.'

National curriculum: Year 1 number and place value (DfE, 2013)

'Pupils should be taught to:

- Count to and across 100, forwards and backwards, beginning with 0 or 1, or from any given number.
- Count, read and write numbers to 100 in numerals; count in multiples of twos, fives and tens.
- Given a number, identify one more and one less.
- Identify and represent numbers using objects and pictorial representations including the number line, and use the language of: equal to, more than, less than (fewer), most, least.
- Read and write numbers from 1 to 20 in numerals and words.'

Questions to check for language development and understanding

 Reporting	 Towards logical reasoning	Predicting	Projecting	Imagining
Identify the components of the images or book | *'What do you see on this page?'* *'How many different representations of 1 / 2 / 3 / 4 can you see? Show me.'* *'Describe the different groups you can see on this page.'* **Refer to detail: the colour and shape, size or position of an object** | *'Which is the biggest/smallest building on this page?'* **Elaboration** **Identify and describe images or scenes from the book** | *'Tell me, what can you see on the "9" page? [You can use any page, but the more on it, the more children can describe. Listen for mathematical language.]'* **Talk about a sequence of events** | *'How does each page change in the book?'*	**Explain a process** | *'What patterns can you spot and why?'* *'How are all of the pages the same? How are they different?'* **Recognise problems and causes** | *'Tell me, is the house "1" even though there are lots of windows?'* *'Can you show me 5 [or any number] in different ways?'* **Recognise casual and dependent relationships** | *'How are the trees the same/ different? Why are the trees counted as different groups?'* *'Which month is number 2? How do you know?'* **Justify judgements and actions** | *'Why are there only 12 scenes? Why does the book stop at 12?'* *'Tell me, how many groups are we looking for this time?'*	**Anticipate or forecast** | *'Which month will come after April? How do you know? Which number will this month be?'* *'Which is the last month? What season is it? What happens in this month?'* *'Tell me, the last page is 12 – what would come next? Is there another month after December?'* **Predict the consequences of actions and events** | *'What else would fit on this picture? How many would we need?'* *'What colour do you think the eighth block will be? Why?'* *'Why are the pages with 9 and 10 orange?'* **Survey for possible alternatives** | *'Tell me, could it be sunny in December?'*	**Project into the experiences, feelings and reactions of others** | *'Tell me, how do you think the children are feeling on the "10" page? Why do you think that?'* *'Tell me, why are all the people together in December, on the "12" page?'* **Reflect on the meaning of experiences** | *'Tell me, how do the pictures change as the seasons change?'* *'Why aren't there any leaves on the trees in November?'* **Project into a situation never experienced** | *'What do you think it's like to be in the snow in December?'* *'How many people are on the railway track on the "8" page? What do you think they are doing and why?'*	**In an imagined context** | Imagine you are the author...   *'Can you make or draw your own page for one of the numbers?'* *'What groups of things will you draw/collect/position? Why?'* *'How many of each will you need and why?'* *'Which month of the year will your page need to be and why?'*

Worked examples

Understanding the world

Past and present

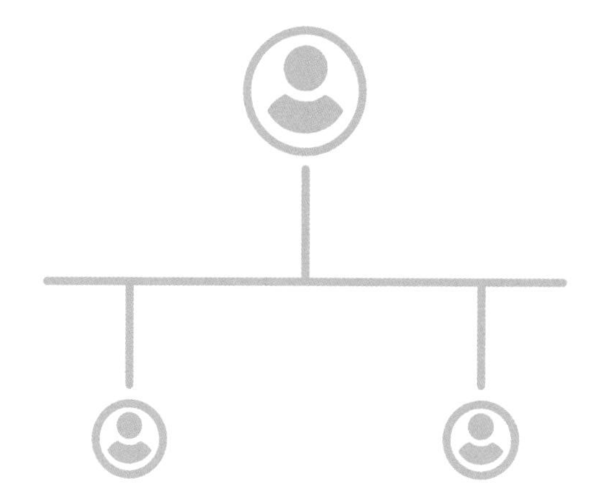

Once There Were Giants by Martin Waddell and Penny Dale

UNDERSTANDING THE WORLD		CHARACTERISTICS OF EFFECTIVE LEARNING
Words to connect = **baby + adult**	Words to connect = **grow + change**	
Self-maintaining Directing Reporting Towards logical reasoning Predicting Projecting Imagining		**PLAYING AND EXPLORING** *Engagement through* • *Finding out and exploring.* • *Playing with what they know.* • *Being willing to 'have a go'.* **ACTIVE LEARNING** *Motivation through* • *Being involved and concentrating.* • *Keeping on trying.* • *Enjoying achieving what they set out to do.* **CREATIVE AND CRITICAL THINKING** *Thinking hard* • *Having their own ideas.* • *Making links.* • *Working with others.*

SPOTLIGHT ON: Understanding the world – past and present

ELG: Past and present (DfE, 2023)

'Children at the expected level of development will:
- Talk about the lives of the people around them and their roles in society.
- Know some similarities and differences between things in the past and now, drawing on their experiences and what has been read in class.
- Understand the past through settings, characters and events encountered in books read in class and storytelling.'

National curriculum: KS1 history (DfE, 2013)

'Pupils should be taught about:
- Changes within living memory. Where appropriate, these should be used to reveal aspects of change in national life.
- Events beyond living memory that are significant nationally or globally (for example, the Great Fire of London, the first aeroplane flight or events commemorated through festivals or anniversaries).
- The lives of significant individuals in the past who have contributed to national and international achievements. Some should be used to compare aspects of life in different periods (for example, Elizabeth I and Queen Victoria, Christopher Columbus and Neil Armstrong, William Caxton and Tim Berners-Lee, Pieter Bruegel the Elder and LS Lowry, Rosa Parks and Emily Davison, Mary Seacole and/or Florence Nightingale and Edith Cavell).
- Significant historical events, people and places in their own locality.'

Questions to check for language development and understanding

 Reporting	Towards logical reasoning	Predicting	Projecting	Imagining
Identify the components of the images or book | *'What do you see on this page?'* *'Who is on this page?'* *'Describe the family [Mum, Dad, Jill, John, Uncle Tom and girl].'* **Refer to detail: the colour and shape, size or position of an object** | *'What colours are the toys? Where are they and why?'* **Elaboration** **Identify and describe images or scenes from the book** | *'Tell me, what is happening here [use page with baby in highchair]?'* **Talk about a sequence of events** | *'What happened in the story? What did we see the child/their family doing?'* *'Tell me about how the child grew up.'*	**Explain a process** | *'What happened as the child got older?'* **Recognise problems and causes** | *'What problem did the girl have when she went to playgroup?'* *'What problem was there when she went to the park to feed the ducks?'* *'How did the girl change when she went to school?'* **Recognise casual and dependent relationships** | *'Why are the girl's family important?'* *'Who did the girl fight with?'* **Justify judgements and actions** | *'Was the girl right to call people names and upset the water on Millie Magee at playgroup?'*	**Anticipate or forecast** | *'Which memory do you think the girl likes best? Why?'* *'What do you think the girl became when she was older?'* **Predict the consequences of actions and events** | *'Explain why there are giants in the house again.'* *'What will happen as the girl's baby gets older?'* **Survey for possible alternatives** | *'What could have happened if Dad had pretended to be something other than a dragon?'*	**Project into the experiences, feelings and reactions of others** | *'Tell me, why did the girl cry?'* *'How do you think the girl felt when her family watched her in the race?'* *'When the girl got married, how do you think her family felt?'* **Project into the reactions of others** | *'How did you feel as you saw the girl change and grow?'* **Project into a situation never experienced** | *'If you were the girl at playgroup, what would you have done?'*	**In an imagined context** | Using puppets, characters or a phone or walkie-talkie.    *'Hello, girl from story. What is your favourite memory?'* *'Hello, Mum. How are you feeling on your daughter's wedding day?'*

Worked examples

Understanding the world

People, culture and communities

The Great Race by Emily Hiles

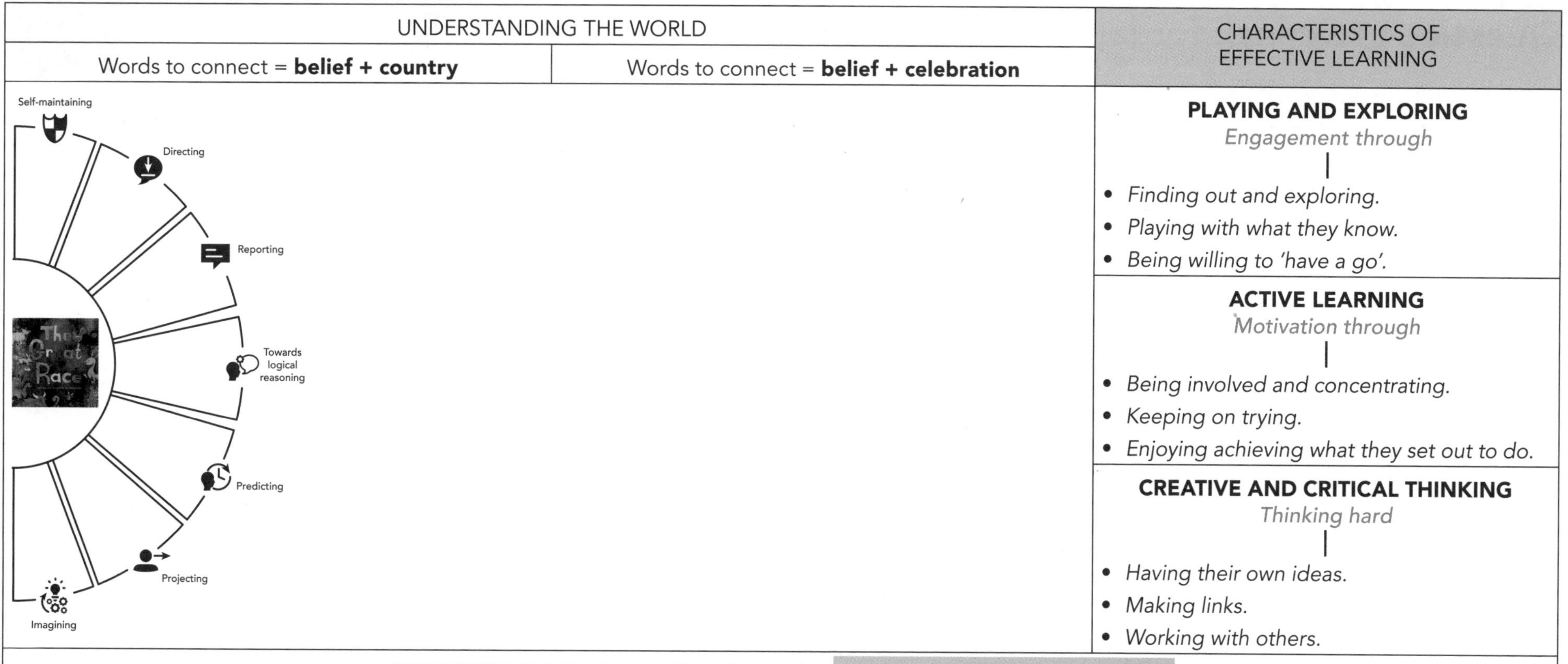

UNDERSTANDING THE WORLD		CHARACTERISTICS OF EFFECTIVE LEARNING
Words to connect = **belief + country**	Words to connect = **belief + celebration**	
		PLAYING AND EXPLORING *Engagement through* • *Finding out and exploring.* • *Playing with what they know.* • *Being willing to 'have a go'.*
		ACTIVE LEARNING *Motivation through* • *Being involved and concentrating.* • *Keeping on trying.* • *Enjoying achieving what they set out to do.*
		CREATIVE AND CRITICAL THINKING *Thinking hard* • *Having their own ideas.* • *Making links.* • *Working with others.*

SPOTLIGHT ON: Understanding the world – people, culture and communities

ELG: People, culture and communities (DfE, 2023)

'Children at the expected level of development will:

- Know some similarities and differences between different religious and cultural communities in this country, drawing on their experiences and what has been read in class.
- Explain some similarities and differences between life in this country and life in other countries, drawing on knowledge from stories, non-fiction texts and – when appropriate – maps.'

KS1/2 respectful relationships (DfE, 2019)

'By the end of primary school, pupils should know:

- The importance of respecting others, even when they are very different from them (for example, physically, in character, personality or backgrounds) or make different choices or have different preferences or beliefs.
- Practical steps they can take in a range of different contexts to improve or support respectful relationships.
- What a stereotype is, and how stereotypes can be unfair, negative or destructive.'

Questions to check for language development and understanding

 Reporting	 Towards logical reasoning	Predicting	Projecting	Imagining
Identify the components of the images or book | *'What do you see on this page?'* *'Who is this? [Jade Emperor]'* *'Describe the [animal].'* *'Rat was smart and small.'* **Refer to detail: the colour and shape, size or position of an object** | *'Describe the Jade Emperor.'* **Elaboration** **Identify and describe images or scenes from the book** | *'Tell me, what happens in this festival?'* **Talk about a sequence of events** | *'What happened in the story?'* *'What did the animals want?'* *'What did the animals have to do?'*	**Explain a process** | *'Why did the Jade Emperor tell the animals to race?'* **Recognise problems and causes** | *'What problem did the animals have?'* *'What problem did the Jade Emperor have?'* *'How did the animals that couldn't swim make it across?'* **Recognise casual and dependent relationships** | *'Why was a race important?'* *'Who was number one?'* **Justify judgements and actions** | *'Was the Jade Emperor right to tell the animals to race? Why do you think that?'*	**Anticipate or forecast** | *'Which animal do you think would win a race across the deep, cold river?'* **Predict the consequences of actions and events** | *'What could have happened if the animals hadn't helped each other?'* *'What if the animals kept on arguing?'* **Survey for possible alternatives** | *'If there wasn't a river, how could the Jade Emperor have arranged the race?'* **Recognition of problems and prediction of solutions** | *'If an animal couldn't swim, what did they do to get across?'*	**Project into the experiences, feelings and reactions of others** | *'Rooster, monkey and goat worked together and arrived on a long log boat.'* *'Tell me, how do you think the animals felt about swimming?'* *'Which animal do you think was the most confident about swimming? What makes you think that?'* **Project into the reactions of others** | *'When all the animals had made it across the river, how do you think the Emperor felt?'* **Project into a situation never experienced** | *'If you were the Jade Emperor, would you worry that some of the animals couldn't swim?'*	**In an imagined context** | Using puppets, characters or a phone or walkie-talkie.    *'Hello, Jade Emperor. Why did you ask the animals to race?'* *'Hello, rat. What other way could you cross the river?'*

Martha Maps It Out by Leigh Hodgkinson

UNDERSTANDING THE WORLD		CHARACTERISTICS OF EFFECTIVE LEARNING
Words to connect = **map + place**	Words to connect = **street + home**	
		PLAYING AND EXPLORING *Engagement through* • *Finding out and exploring.* • *Playing with what they know.* • *Being willing to 'have a go'.*
		ACTIVE LEARNING *Motivation through* • *Being involved and concentrating.* • *Keeping on trying.* • *Enjoying achieving what they set out to do.*
		CREATIVE AND CRITICAL THINKING *Thinking hard* • *Having their own ideas.* • *Making links.* • *Working with others.*

SPOTLIGHT ON: Understanding the world – people, culture and communities

ELG: People, culture and communities (DfE, 2023)

'Children at the expected level of development will:

- Describe their immediate environment using knowledge from observation, discussion, stories, non-fiction texts and maps.
- Explain some similarities and differences between life in this country and life in other countries, drawing on knowledge from stories, non-fiction texts and – when appropriate – maps.'

National curriculum: KS1 geographical skills and fieldwork (DfE, 2013)

'Pupils should be taught to:

- Use world maps, atlases and globes to identify the United Kingdom and its countries, as well as the countries, continents and oceans studied at this key stage.
- Use simple compass directions (North, South, East, West) and locational/directional language (e.g. near and far; left and right) to describe the location of features and routes on a map.
- Use aerial photographs and plan perspectives to recognise landmarks and basic human and physical features; devise a simple map; and use and construct basic symbols in a key.
- Use simple fieldwork and observational skills to study the geography of their school and its grounds and the key human and physical features of its surrounding environment.'

Questions to check for language development and understanding

Reporting	Towards logical reasoning	Predicting	Projecting	Imagining
Identify the components of the images or book | *'What do you see on this page?'* *'Who is on this page?'* *'Describe Martha's bedroom.'* **Refer to detail: the colour and shape, size or position of an object** | *'What colours are the different rooms in Martha's house?'* **Elaboration** **Identify and describe images or scenes from the book** | *'Tell me, what can you see in Martha's city? What buildings/ features are there?'* **Talk about a sequence of events** | *'What journey does Martha take us on?'* *'What do we learn about Martha?* *'Tell me about where Martha lives.'*	**Explain a process** | *'What different maps did Martha draw? Why?'* *'Were they all maps of places? Explain.'* **Recognise problems and causes** | *'Does everybody live in the same sort of home?'* *'Would everyone draw similar maps to Martha? Why/why not?'* **Recognise casual and dependent relationships** | *'What would be on your maps? Why?'* **Justify judgements and actions** | *'Which one of Martha's maps do you prefer? Why?'*	**Anticipate or forecast** | *'Which map do you think is most important to Martha?'* **Predict the consequences of actions and events** | *'What do you think Martha will draw a map of next?'* *'Can you think of any other adventures Martha might have?'* *'How might Martha's maps change as she grows up?'* **Survey for possible alternatives** | *'If Martha lived in a different place and a different house, how would that change the map?'*	**Project into the experiences, feelings and reactions of others** | *'Tell me, why did Martha draw a map of herself?'* *'How do you think Martha feels about space? Why?'* **Reflect on the meaning of experiences** | *'How do you think Martha would feel if she shared her art with everyone [show page in book]?'* **Project into a situation never experienced** | *'Look at the world map. Where might you like to visit? Why?'*	**In an imagined context** | Using puppets, characters or a phone or walkie-talkie, or the role-play area. *'Tell me, which one of Martha's adventures would you most like to go on and why?'* *'Let's pretend to be on that adventure.'* *'Tell me about your map. What adventure is it taking you on?'* *'Let's make a telescope – what can you see through your telescope?'*

Worked examples

Understanding the world

Natural world

Similarities and differences, seasons and changes

UNDERSTANDING THE WORLD		CHARACTERISTICS OF EFFECTIVE LEARNING
Words to connect = **autumn + fall**	Words to connect = **seasons + change**	

Self-maintaining
Directing
Reporting
Towards logical reasoning
Predicting
Projecting
Imagining

PLAYING AND EXPLORING

Engagement through

- *Finding out and exploring.*
- *Playing with what they know.*
- *Being willing to 'have a go'.*

ACTIVE LEARNING

Motivation through

- *Being involved and concentrating.*
- *Keeping on trying.*
- *Enjoying achieving what they set out to do.*

CREATIVE AND CRITICAL THINKING

Thinking hard

- *Having their own ideas.*
- *Making links.*
- *Working with others.*

SPOTLIGHT ON: Understanding the world – natural world

ELG: The natural world (DfE, 2023)

'Children at the expected level of development will:

- Explore the natural world around them, making observations and drawing pictures of animals and plants.
- Know some similarities and differences between the natural world around them and contrasting environments, drawing on their experiences and what has been read in class.
- Understand some important processes and changes in the natural world around them, including the seasons and changing states of matter.'

National curriculum: Year 1 seasonal changes/plants (DfE, 2013)

'Pupils should be taught to:

- Observe changes across the four seasons.
- Observe and describe weather associated with the seasons and how day length varies.
- Identify and name a variety of common wild and garden plants, including deciduous and evergreen trees.
- Identify and describe the basic structure of a variety of common flowering plants, including trees.'

Questions to check for language development and understanding

 Reporting	Towards logical reasoning	Predicting	Projecting	Imagining
Talk about a sequence of events *'Tell me about the seasons.'* *'What follows winter? What season are we in now? How do you know?'* **Refer to detail: the colour and shape, size or position of an object/character** *'What is spring [summer, autumn, winter] like?'* *'Tell me about how plants change throughout the seasons.'* **Elaboration** **Identify and describe images or scenes from the book.** *'What is a season?'* *'What's the difference between the leaves? Describe the leaves of these two plants.'* *'Tell me about months.'* **Absence of conditions** *'Why do the leaves fall?'*	**Explain a process** *'What season happens after this one?'* *'Does the garden always look the same?'* **Recognise casual and dependent relationships** *'How do plants change through the seasons?'* **Recognise problems and causes** *'Does autumn happen at the same time around the world?'* **Justify judgements and actions** *'Which season do you prefer? Why?'* *'How do the words **season** and **change** join?'*	**Anticipate or forecast** *'Soon it will be spring – what will we see?'* *'What do we need to wear outside today? Would that change?'* *'What will change in the summer?'* **Survey for possible alternatives** *'What would happen if it was summer every day? What would change?'* **Predict the consequences of actions and events** *'What if it stayed hot all year round?'* **Recognition of problems and solutions** *'It's raining – what do you need to wear outside.'* *'How do we look after ourselves in different seasons?'*	**Project into the experiences, feelings and reactions of others** *'How do we help the animals and plants in our gardens? Why do we do that?'* *'In winter, what could we do to help the birds in our gardens? Why?'* **Project into the reactions of others** *'If you saw someone standing on a plant, what would you do?'* **Project into a situation never experienced** *'If you were a seed and you were planted in the winter, how would you feel?'*	**In an imagined context** Using puppets, characters or a phone or walkie-talkie.    *'What can you see through your binoculars? What season are you seeing?'* *'I'm looking through my binoculars and can see…'*

Worked examples

Expressive arts and design

Creating with materials

Luna Loves Art by Joseph Coelho and Fiona Lumbers

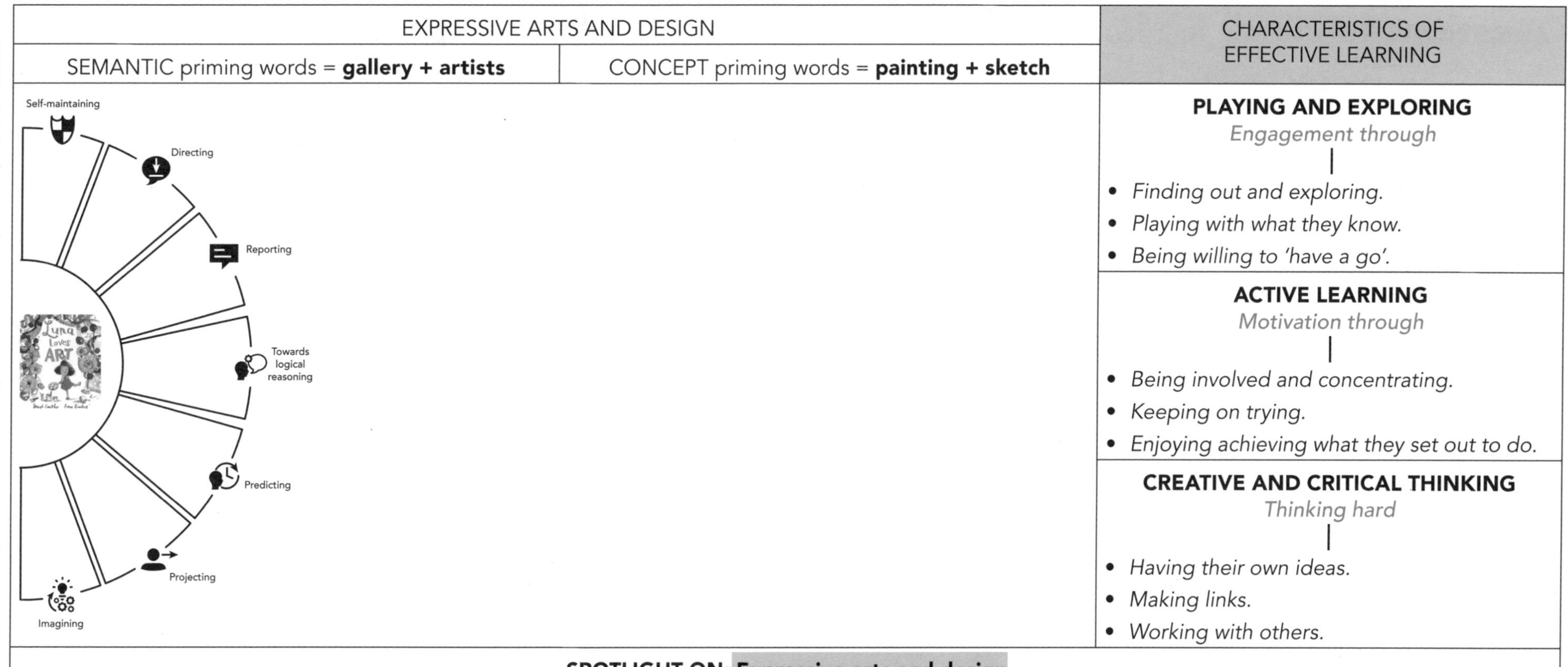

EXPRESSIVE ARTS AND DESIGN		CHARACTERISTICS OF EFFECTIVE LEARNING
SEMANTIC priming words = **gallery + artists**	CONCEPT priming words = **painting + sketch**	

PLAYING AND EXPLORING
Engagement through

- *Finding out and exploring.*
- *Playing with what they know.*
- *Being willing to 'have a go'.*

ACTIVE LEARNING
Motivation through

- *Being involved and concentrating.*
- *Keeping on trying.*
- *Enjoying achieving what they set out to do.*

CREATIVE AND CRITICAL THINKING
Thinking hard

- *Having their own ideas.*
- *Making links.*
- *Working with others.*

SPOTLIGHT ON: Expressive arts and design

ELG: Creating with materials (DfE, 2023)

'Children at the expected level of development will:

- Safely use and explore a variety of materials, tools and techniques, experimenting with colour, design, texture, form and function.
- Share their creations, explaining the process they have used.'

National curriculum: KS1 art and design (DfE, 2013)

'Pupils should be taught:

- To use a range of materials creatively to design and make products.
- To use drawing, painting and sculpture to develop and share their ideas, experiences and imagination.
- To develop a wide range of art and design techniques in using colour, pattern, texture, line, shape, form and space.
- About the work of a range of artists, craft makers and designers, describing the differences and similarities between different practices and disciplines.'

Questions to check for language development and understanding

 Reporting	 Towards logical reasoning	 Predicting	 Projecting	 Imagining
Identify the components of the images or book | *'Tell me, what is happening here? Who is this? What are they doing?'* **Refer to detail: the colour and shape, size or position of an object** | *'How would you describe the tiger in the jungle?'* **Talk about a sequence of events** | *'What happened here? Why?'* *'What does the teacher do? Why?'* **Reflect on the meaning of experiences** | *'Miss Rosa takes the class to a dark room, full of lights and sounds. How did you feel when the children were in that room?'*	**Explain a process** | *'How did they get to the art gallery? Where did they go in the art gallery?'* *'What were they there to see? What did they see?'* *'What different materials have the artists used to create the art that Luna and Finn see?'* **Recognise casual and dependent relationships** | *'How did Mum make Luna feel better after Finn scrunched up her sketch?'* *'What did Mum do to help Finn?'* **Recognise problems and causes** | *'Why do you think Finn might have been feeling angry/sad?'* **Justify judgements and actions** | *'Tell me about when you have created a piece of art that you have been really proud of. What materials did you use? What materials do you enjoy using in your classroom? Why?'* *'Do you think you would like to visit the art gallery? Why?'*	**Anticipate or forecast** | *'I wonder what Finn and Luna talk about on the bus on the way back to school?'* *'What art do you think they might create when they get back to their classroom?'* **Predict the consequences of actions and events** | *'If Luna had got cross with Finn for scrunching up her sketch, what do you think might have happened?'* *'What do you think Finn's teacher, Miss Rosa, said to him when she took him aside?'* **Survey for possible alternatives** | *'What might have happened if Miss Rosa and Mum did not speak with Finn?'*	**Project into the experiences, feelings and reactions of others** | *'Tell me, what might Luna tell Dad when she gets home from school?'* *'Why did Luna say "Hey!" to Finn?'* **Project into a situation never experienced** | *'If you went to the same art gallery for the first time, what would you want to look at first? Why?'*	**In an imagined context** | Using puppets, characters or a phone or walkie-talkie, or the role-play area.    *'Hello, Luna and Finn. What paintings are you going to show us today?'* *'Can you pretend to be an artist, like the artists whose work Finn and Luna saw in the gallery? What might you create? What materials could you use?'*

Structured story time from CUSP Early Foundations

Early years structured story time

Age: 4-5 years

Text	Luna Loves Art by Joseph Coelho and Fiona Lumbers	
Text introduction	This story is about a girl called Luna and a boy called Finn. They go on a school trip to an art gallery. Finn has a difficult time and Luna struggles with this, but her mum helps him. In the end, they all enjoy their trip.	
Vocabulary (tier 2)	alone, huge/massive, sketch, scrunches, aside, describe, thrashing, wanders	
Language to draw attention to while reading	'instant camera'; 'Impressionist and Post-Impressionist Rooms'; 'flowers look alive'; 'Abstract Paintings Room'; 'Kazimir Malevich's "Black Square" is all edged, black and cracked. A night-time robbed of stars, A phone waiting to ring'; 'pulsing lights'	
Context teaching	*'School trips – what are they?' 'Have you been on a school trip?' 'Art gallery – what is an art gallery?' 'Has anyone been to an art gallery?' 'Who has seen art by different artists [show examples]?' 'What sort of art do you like creating?' 'Have you got any favourite pictures?' 'What does it feel like to be the new person at school?' 'How did you feel when you started school?'*	
At the end of this unit, pupils will...	**Know:**	**Be able to:**
	• What an art gallery is. • That there are lots of different artists who create in different ways. • That not all families are the same.	• Engage in extended conversations about stories, learning new vocabulary. • Talk about a character's feelings, assigning the correct vocabulary to emotions. • Empathise with characters (starting school, different families).

Lesson 1	
Vocabulary	*'Let's explore some of the interesting words from our story today.'* My turn / your turn / 'alone' (x 3). 'Alone' means having no one else with you. My turn / your turn / 'huge' / 'massive' (x 3). Connect the two words: 'huge' and 'massive' have very similar meanings as they both mean 'very big'. The words could be ordered in terms of shades of meaning (big, large, huge, massive) to connect to other words pupils may know.
Fluency/oracy/ drama	*'Let's practise the first page together. Copy my voice [echo-reading]: Luna Loves Art. Today she is going on a school trip. School trip backpack – check! School trip lunch box – check! School trip instant camera – click!'* Emphasise key words: *'How do we say "loves", "today", "check" and "click"? Why do we say them like that? I wonder if there are any more "clicks" to read in the story?'*
Reading the text	Read and enjoy the text, discussing key language as you go. Point out the words 'huge' and 'massive'. Point out the different types of art/different artists whose work the children see.
Thinking harder	*'Do you think Finn enjoyed being at the art gallery? Why/why not? Talk to your partner.'*

Lesson 2	
Vocabulary	*'Before we start reading, let's look at some more interesting words from our book.'* My turn / your turn / 'sketch' (x 3). *'In the story it says, "Luna does a sketch...Scribble!" A sketch is a drawing. Can you think of another sentence that we can say with the word "sketch" in it? Talk to your partner.'* My turn / your turn / 'scrunches' (x 3). *'"Finn scrunches up Luna's picture!" Model what "scrunches" means. Can you make up your own sentence with the word "scrunches" in it? Talk to your partner.'*
Fluency/oracy/ drama	Echo-read parts of the text that relate to Finn. My turn / your turn / 'Finn is alone'. My turn / your turn / 'But Finn doesn't care. Finn is looking down'. Talk about how you read these parts and why you use a low/sad voice.
Reading the text	Read the text again, encouraging pupils to join in with parts that they recognise ('Luna takes a photo…Click!'). Talk about Finn's emotions as you read.
Thinking harder	*'How do you think Finn feels about the art that they see? Talk to your partner. What is your favourite piece of art? Why? Talk to your partner.'*
Lesson 3	
Vocabulary	*'Our interesting words today are "aside" and "describe". They sound a little bit like each other, but one has "ide" at the end and one has "ibe".'* My turn / your turn / 'aside' (x 3). *'"Aside" means to take someone out of the way or to one side. Miss Rosa takes Finn away from the group.'* My turn / your turn / 'describe'. *'If we describe something, we say what it is like.'*
Fluency/oracy/ drama	*'In pairs, show me what it looks like to take someone aside gently.'* First, discuss how this could be done, then act it out physically, using a caring arm around the person. Say 'Miss Rosa takes Finn aside'. Then swap so each child has a turn at being Finn/Miss Rosa.
Reading the text	Read the text again. Explore Luna's emotions across the story: *'When does Luna feel unhappy/confused?'*
Thinking harder	*'Choose one of the paintings from the story to describe. Talk to your partner – what is it like?'* Remind pupils what 'describe' means.
Lesson 4	
Vocabulary	*'Our special words from our story today are "thrashing" and "wanders". We are going to think about where we might use them.'* My turn / your turn / 'thrashing' (x 3). *'The wind was thrashing through the trees; the rain was thrashing down.'* My turn / your turn / 'wanders' (x 3). *'The tiger wanders the jungle; the horse wanders through the grass; the girl wanders through the park alone.'*
Fluency/oracy/ drama	Freeze-frame Finn and Luna when they first get to the gallery and then again when they leave the gallery. What is the difference? Make comparisons. Look at pictures to support thinking.
Reading the text	Reread the story – look at the differences between Finn's and Luna's reactions to the tiger painting. *'Why does Finn say these things about the tiger painting?'*
Thinking harder	*'How do Luna and Luna's mum help Finn in the story? Talk to your partner. Do you think Finn is a good/bad character? Why? Talk to your partner.'*
Lesson 5	
Probing questions for thinking harder in provision	*'Can you create art like one of the artists from the story? What materials will you use? Is art just paintings and drawings? What is your favourite material to create with and why? Which tools do you find the most useful and why? Which tools do you think this artist has used to create those shapes?'*

An example of progression from CUSP Early Foundations

CUSP art and design and design technology / early years foundational knowledge / expressive arts and design

'The development of children's artistic and cultural awareness supports their imagination and creativity. It is important that children have regular opportunities to engage with the arts, enabling them to explore and play with a wide range of media and materials. The quality and variety of what children see, hear and participate in is crucial for developing their understanding, self-expression, vocabulary and ability to communicate through the arts. The frequency, repetition and depth of their experiences are fundamental to their progress in interpreting and appreciating what they hear, respond to and observe' (DfE, 2023)

Pupil starting points

It is important that we make no assumptions about what pupils do or do not know on entry to our settings. The relationships we build with our pupils are fundamental to understanding and developing them as individuals, with deep knowledge of their context through positive relationships with parents/carers and robust transition procedures such as home visits and baseline systems. The below is an 'indicator' of what we might expect our pupils to know, linked to *Birth to 5 Matters* (Early Education, 2021) and *Development Matters* (DfE, 2021) and the progress check at age 2.

In expressive arts and design, pupils may have experience of: experimenting with ways to enclose a space, creating shapes, playing with colour (for example, combining colours), using 3D and 2D structures to explore materials, mark-making with a variety of media, exploring paint using body parts as well as brushes and other tools, exploring different materials, and making simple models that express their ideas. Through observation and interaction, we can find out what our pupils already know and can do, and can use the below to build on this.

	2-3 years	3-4 years	4-5 years	ELGs	National curriculum
Structured story time linked text	***Wow! Said the Owl* by Tim Hopgood**	***The Dot* by Peter H. Reynolds**	***Luna Loves Art* by Joseph Coelho and Fiona Lumbers**	ELG: Creating with materials (DfE, 2023) 'Children at the expected level of developmental will: • Safely use and explore a variety of materials, tools and techniques, experimenting with colour, design, texture, form and function.'	KS1 art and design (DfE, 2013) 'Pupils should be taught: • To use a range of materials creatively to design and make products • To use drawing, painting and sculpture to develop and share their ideas, experiences and imagination • To develop a wide range of art and design techniques in using colour, pattern, texture, line, shape, form and space.'
Range of materials	• Explore different materials, using all of their senses to investigate them. • Manipulate and play with different materials. • Use their imagination as they consider what they can do with different materials. • Use block play to begin to build and design.	• Explore different materials freely, to develop their ideas about how to use them and what to make. • Join different materials, beginning to explain choice linked to shape and texture/properties. • Use various construction materials, e.g. joining pieces, stacking vertically and horizontally, balancing, making enclosures and creating spaces.	• Develop their own ideas through experimentation with a diverse range of materials. • Increasingly choose more appropriate materials for the job, e.g. cotton reels/lids for wheels, wool/thread for hair. • Join different materials explaining why they have chosen a specific fixing. • Purposefully choose construction materials for a specific job.		

'The CUSP team have developed a thoughtful and ambitious EYFS curriculum, which I'm sure will help practitioners to prepare early years children well for their future learning'

Gill Jones MBE, group chief quality officer and safeguarding lead, Busy Bees

William Bee's Wonderful World of Things That Go!

EXPRESSIVE ARTS AND DESIGN		CHARACTERISTICS OF EFFECTIVE LEARNING
SEMANTIC priming words = **garage + vehicle**	CONCEPT priming words = **truck + lorry**	

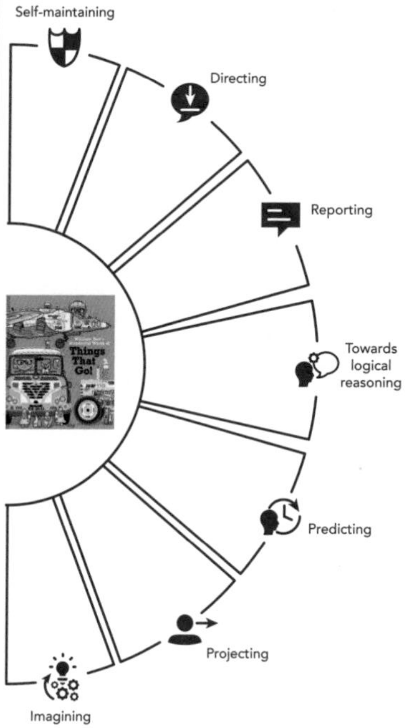

Self-maintaining
Directing
Reporting
Towards logical reasoning
Predicting
Projecting
Imagining

PLAYING AND EXPLORING
Engagement through

- *Finding out and exploring.*
- *Playing with what they know.*
- *Being willing to 'have a go'.*

ACTIVE LEARNING
Motivation through

- *Being involved and concentrating.*
- *Keeping on trying.*
- *Enjoying achieving what they set out to do.*

CREATIVE AND CRITICAL THINKING
Thinking hard

- *Having their own ideas.*
- *Making links.*
- *Working with others.*

SPOTLIGHT ON: Design and technology

ELG: Creating with materials (DfE, 2023)

'Children at the expected level of development will:

- Safely use and explore a variety of materials, tools and techniques, experimenting with colour, design, texture, form and function.
- Share their creations, explaining the process they have used.'

National curriculum: KS1 design and technology (DfE, 2013)

'When designing and making, pupils should be taught to:

- Design purposeful, functional, appealing products for themselves and other users based on design criteria.
- Generate, develop, model and communicate their ideas through talking, drawing, templates, mock-ups and, where appropriate, information and communication technology.
- Explore and evaluate a range of existing products.'

Questions to check for language development and understanding

Any section of *Things That Go!* could be used and the questions adapted. We have used 'trucks' as most children will have seen trucks.

Reporting	 Towards logical reasoning	 Predicting	Projecting	Imagining
Elaboration **Identify and describe images or scenes from the book** *'Tell me, what can you see in this picture [first double-page spread]. Where might he be?'* **Refer to detail: the colour and shape, size or position of an object/character** *'What does William Bee look like?'* *'Describe the fuel tanker/coal-fired stream truck/amphibian truck.'* **Talk about a sequence of events** *'What did William Bee drive after the amphibian truck?'* *'Why does he need the racing car transporter?'* **Absence of conditions** *'What would happen if we didn't have trucks?'* **Reflect on the meaning of experiences** *'Why do we need trucks to carry the bricks, wood and pipes?'*	**Explain a process** *'How do the trucks move? What do they need?'* *'How does the truck that carries the bricks, wood and pipes lift them?'* *'How does the concrete mixer work?'* *'How does the coal-fired steam truck work?'* **Recognise casual and dependent relationships** *'Why is the fuel truck important?'* *'What will the coffee truck need in it? Why?'* **Recognise problems and causes** *'Why might the jet-powered truck be dangerous?'* *'Why did the truck need rescuing?'* **Justify judgements and actions** *'Why did William Bee rescue the truck?'* *'What did he need to do to rescue the truck?'*	**Anticipate or forecast** *'I wonder what happens when there is a fire?'* *'Tell me, where would the concrete mixer be useful? Why?'* **Survey for possible alternatives** *'What else could William Bee have turned the rescued truck into instead of a snow-blowing truck?'* **Predict the consequences of actions and events** *'What would happen if any of the trucks broke down?'* *'How could William Bee help?'* **Recognition of problems and solutions** *'Why might we need an amphibious truck?'*	**Project into the experiences, feelings and reactions of others** *'Which truck do you think William Bee finds most useful and why?'* *'Which truck do you think is his favourite and why?'* *'Which truck is most useful to us in our country/community? Why?'* *'What will William Bee need in his seaside truck? Why?'* **Project into a situation never experienced** *'Do we need a snow-blowing truck in this country? Why/why not?'*	**In an imagined context** Using puppets, characters or a phone or walkie-talkie.    *'Hello, William Bee. Which truck is most useful for lifting things? Why?'* *'Hello, William Bee. What can you make me in your coffee truck? What revolting things are on the specials menu today?'* *'Hello, this is William Bee. Can you design a new truck for me that carries sand and tips it out?'* *'Pretend to be William Bee rescuing the truck at the scrap yard. What do you need to do? Can you show me and use words to describe what you are doing?'* *'Can you design and make a different truck for William Bee? What job will your truck do?'*

Worked examples

Expressive arts and design

Being imaginative and expressive

The Story Orchestra by Jessica Courtney-Tickle

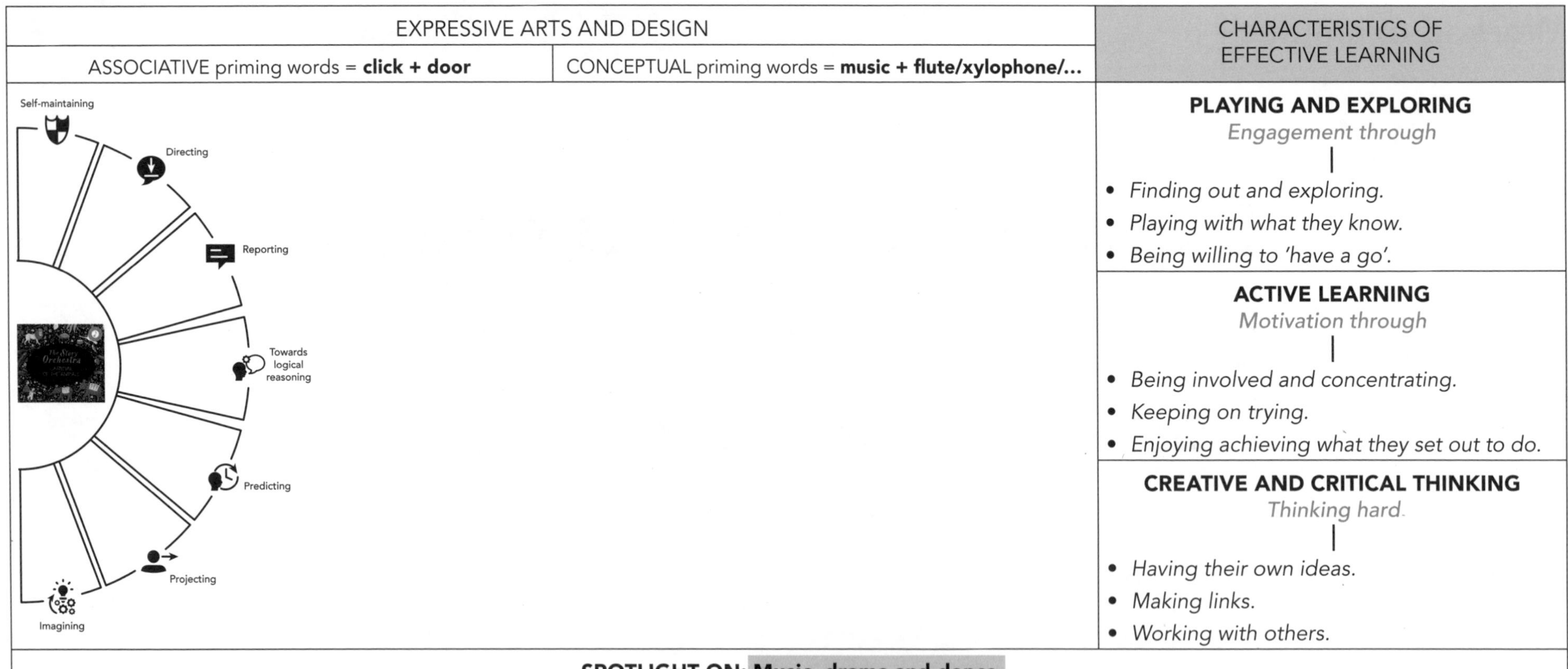

SPOTLIGHT ON: Music, drama and dance

ELG: Being imaginative and expressive (DfE, 2023)

'Children at the expected level of development will:

- Invent, adapt and recount narratives and stories with peers and their teacher.
- Sing a range of well-known nursery rhymes and songs.
- Perform songs, rhymes, poems and stories with others, and – when appropriate – try to move in time with music.'

National curriculum: KS1 music (DfE, 2013)

'Pupils should be taught to:

- Use their voices expressively and creatively by singing songs and speaking chants and rhymes.
- Play tuned and untuned instruments musically.
- Listen with concentration and understanding to a range of high-quality live and recorded music.
- Experiment with, create, select and combine sounds using the inter-related dimensions of music.'

Questions to check for language development and understanding

 Reporting	 Towards logical reasoning	 Predicting	Projecting	Imagining
Refer to a sequence of events | *'What animals did Thomas and James meet?'* *'Thomas and James found a secret door – what happened next?'* *'What did Thomas find after the brothers met the lion?'* **Label the component parts of a scene** | *'Tell me, what can you see here [pointing at the elephant with the blue hat]?'* **Elaborate and refer to detail: the colour and shape, size or position of an object** | *'What can you see on this page? Describe what the dinosaurs are like.'* **Talk about an incident** | *'Tell me, what happens when the brothers get to the ocean?'* **Reflect on the meanings of experiences, including feelings** | *'How did you feel when the brothers met the lion?'*	**Recognise casual and dependent relationships** | *'How does the music on each page connect to the animals?'* *'Why do you think the tortoise is called Lonely George?'* *'Which music do you think is really good – what page is that on? Why is that?'* *'Why do you think the xylophone is the main instrument you hear on the dinosaur page?'* *'Does every place the boys visit have the main instrument drawn on the page?'* **Recognise problems and causes** | *'What problem did the boys solve with the birds?'* *'Who helped them?'* *'How did they help?'* **Justify judgements and actions** | *'Let's think about those birds in a cage. What would you do if you found those birds?'* *'When might it be OK for birds to be in a cage?'*	**Anticipate or forecast** | *'I wonder what happens when the boys leave the tortoise called Lonely George?'* *'What do you think Lonely George might have done when the boys leave, on his birthday?'* **Predict the consequences of actions and events** | *'The friendly dolphin took James for an underwater ride. What do you think Thomas did at the same time?'* *'What could have gone wrong when the brothers were underwater?'* **Survey for possible alternatives** | *'What other sounds do you think would go well with the elephants?'* *'If the dolphin hadn't come along, what other animal could have done the same job?'* *'What might have happened if all the animals had gone back through the secret door with Thomas and James?'*	**Project into the experiences, feelings and reactions of others** | *'How does the music on the swan page make you feel?'* *'Why do you think that instrument [flute] was chosen?'* *'How does Lonely George feel when he meets the boys?'* *'Do you think Lonely George's feelings change when the boys leave?'* *'Do the dinosaurs want to be scary?'* *'What instruments do you like listening to? Why is that?'* **Project into a situation never experienced** | *'If you were James on the dolphin, how do you think you might feel? Why?'* *'Even though the dinosaurs look scary, how would you help them?'*	**In an imagined context** | *'What places would you add to the story?'* *'What animals would you see there?'* *'What sounds do you think would go with that place/animal?'* *'Pretend to be James or Thomas – where might you go and visit? Why?'*  *'Hello, it's the lion here. The animals want to play a game with me. Can you tell them when to hide on different pages and then I will look for them.'* *'Where would you help the elephants to hide?'* *'Where would you help Lonely George to hide? What about the birds?'*

Progression and thematic mapping of more beautiful books

Age 2-3

I Want to Be... series Becky Davies	**Favourite Nursery Rhymes** Ladybird	**Ravi's Roar** Tom Percival	**Dear Zoo** Rod Campbell	**Billy and The Beast** Nadia Shireen
Oi Frog! Kes Gray	**Nursery? Not Today!** Rebecca Patterson	**Oliver's Vegetables** Vivian French	**Hey, Water!** Antoinette Portis	**Rain Before Rainbows** Smriti Halls
The Big Book of Kindness Pat-a-Cake	**My First Heroes series** Campbell Books	**Goldilocks and the Three Bears** Mara Alperin	**Lost and Found** Oliver Jeffers	**Meg and Mog** Helen Nicoll
Funnybones Janet & Allan Ahlberg	**You Choose** Pippa Goodhart	**People Need People** Benjamin Zephaniah	**In Every House, On Every Street** Jess Hitchman	**Who Are You?** Smriti Halls
Elephant in my Kitchen! Smriti Halls	**Come Over to My House** Eliza Hull & Sally Rippin	**I Want My Hat Back** Jon Klassen	**Wow! Said the Owl** Tim Hopgood	**Mabel and the Mountain** Kim Hillyard

Favourite Nursery Rhymes (Ladybird)
Head, Shoulders, Knees and Toes; Incy Wincy Spider; Humpty Dumpty; Twinkle, Twinkle; Row, Row, Row Your Boat; Wheels on the Bus

Key themes
- Revisiting authors
- Heritage texts /traditional tales/classic
- Diversity of representation – author or protagonists
- Strong female role model
- Specific social, ethical, moral issues/PSED
- Curriculum links

Age 3-4

The Dot Peter H. Reynolds	**Favourite Nursery Rhymes** Ladybird	**All Through the Night** Polly Faber	**The Same But Different Too** Karl Newson	**The Extraordinary Gardener** Sam Boughton
I Am Nefertiti Annemarie Anang	**What Happened to You?** James Catchpole	**Splash** Claire Cashmore	**The Good Egg** Jory John	**Astro Girl** Ken Wilson-Max
The Worrysaurus Rachel Bright	**Tidy** Emily Gravett	**Errol's Garden** Gillian Hibbs	**A Great Big Cuddle** Michael Rosen	**The Queen's Hat** Steve Antony
The Three Little Pigs Mara Alperin	**The Body Book** Hannah Alice	**My Hair** Hannah Lee	**Tiddler** Julia Donaldson	**The Suitcase** Chris Naylor-Ballesteros
Home is Where the Birds Sing Cynthia Rylant	**Do Baby Elephants Suck Their Trunks?** Ben Lerwill	**My Family and Other Families** Richard & Lewis Edwards-Middleton	**The Way Back Home** Oliver Jeffers	**You Choose Fairy Tales** Pippa Goodhart

Favourite Nursery Rhymes (Ladybird)
Hey Diddle Diddle; Five Little Ducks; Hickory Dickory Dock; Five Currant Buns; Miss Polly

Key themes
- Revisiting authors
- Heritage texts /traditional tales/classic
- Diversity of representation – author or protagonists
- Strong female role model
- Specific social, ethical, moral issues/PSED
- Curriculum links

Age 4-5

Bear Shaped Dawn Coulter-Cruttenden	**The Invisible** Tom Percival	**The Squirrels Who Squabbled** Rachel Bright	**Each Peach Pear Plum** Janet & Allan Ahlberg	**What Makes Me a Me?** Matt Goodfellow
Shu Lin's Grandpa Ben Faulks	**Pumpkin Soup** Helen Cooper	**Mrs Noah's Garden** Jackie Morris	**Winnie-the-Pooh Helps the Bees!** Catherine Shoolbred	**The Dark** Lemony Snicket
Luna Loves Art Joseph Coelho	**It's a No-Money Day** Kate Milner	**I'm (Almost) Always Kind** Anna Milbourne	**The Story Orchestra** Katy Flint	**Standing Up to Racism** Dr Pragya Agarwal
The Gingerbread Man Mara Alperin	**Anansi and the Golden Pot** Taiye Selasi	**Celebrations Around The World** Katy Halford	**William Bee's Things That Go!** William Bee	**Tad** Benji Davies
Clean Up! Nathan Bryon	**Mr Wolf's Pancakes** Jan Fearnley	**Martha Maps It Out** Leigh Hodgkinson	**The Wonder** Faye Hanson	**Chicken Clicking** Jeanne Willis & Tony Ross

Favourite Nursery Rhymes (Ladybird)
Ten Green Bottles; Hot Cross Buns; One Potato...; Old Mother Hubbard; Jack and Jill

Key themes
- Revisiting authors
- Heritage texts /traditional tales/classic
- Diversity of representation – author or protagonists
- Strong female role model
- Specific social, ethical, moral issues/PSED
- Curriculum links

We are incredibly proud of our CUSP literature spines for the EYFS and Years 1-6. They are possibly the most ambitious and thoughtfully constructed literature spines in the world and we know they have an impact. Take a look at our evidence-led, teacher-facing resources that also support CUSP Early Foundations: www.unity-curriculum.co.uk/more-information

Ask yourself...

If you were asked these questions, how would you answer?

1. How coherent is planning to enhance the provision, experiences and opportunities children have, with a focus on language development?

2. What opportunities are there for language enhancement through sustained shared thinking experiences?

3. How well do the opportunities and experiences that children engage in support their language development? How are tasks designed to support the development of communication and language?

4. What consistency do staff have in precision questioning to consolidate or sophisticate children's language at the point of learning? How effective are interactions at extending pupils' language development?

5. How deliberate are your choices to ensure that continuous and enhanced provision maximises the impact of language development?

Chapter 6

Monitoring and evaluation

A process to evaluate the language of learning

Opportunity and provision

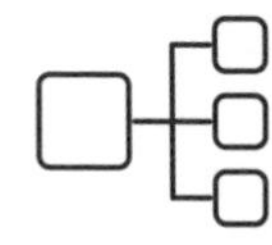
Curriculum expectations, structure and sequence

1. MONITOR

How well does learning endure?

What is helping?

What is hindering?

2. PRIME

Books/sequences/provision

This gives us the opportunity to find out about the vocabulary and concepts children understand. How well do they select words to convey meaning and make sense of the content?

Physical cues

3. STRUCTURED CONVERSATIONS THROUGH SUSTAINED SHARED THINKING

Responding to relevant questioning.

This showcases responses through engagement, questioning and curiosity.

4. EVALUATE

Retrieval and use of vocabulary.

This tells us how well children retain, explain and describe.

Listening tells us about the developmental stage of the children's language.

Knowing and experiencing

Playing and exploring

Children investigate and experience things, and 'have a go'

Active learning

Children concentrate and keep on trying if they encounter difficulties; they enjoy achievements

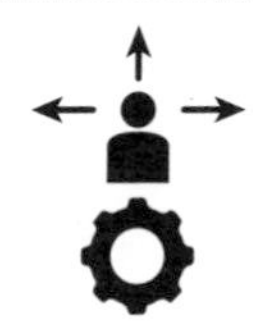

Opportunity

Frequent and varied chances for children to rehearse and develop understanding

Communication and language

Personal, social and emotional development

Physical development

Literacy

Mathematics

Understanding the world

Expressive arts and design

Provision

What children access to develop their understanding

Using what you know

Creating and thinking critically

Children have and develop their own ideas, make links between ideas, and develop strategies for doing things

Helping the rest of the school to understand the EYFS

To ensure the curriculum is coherent and cumulative from the moment children join the school, we need to make it easy for every staff member to know and understand the choices made. For some subject leaders, it can be a challenge to explain what happens in the EYFS succinctly and with precision.

The grids on the following pages have helped non-specialist subject leaders to know more and use that knowledge to champion subjects that include the EYFS from the outset. The grids help to connect the educational programmes, ELGs and the national curriculum; if you find them useful, please use them.

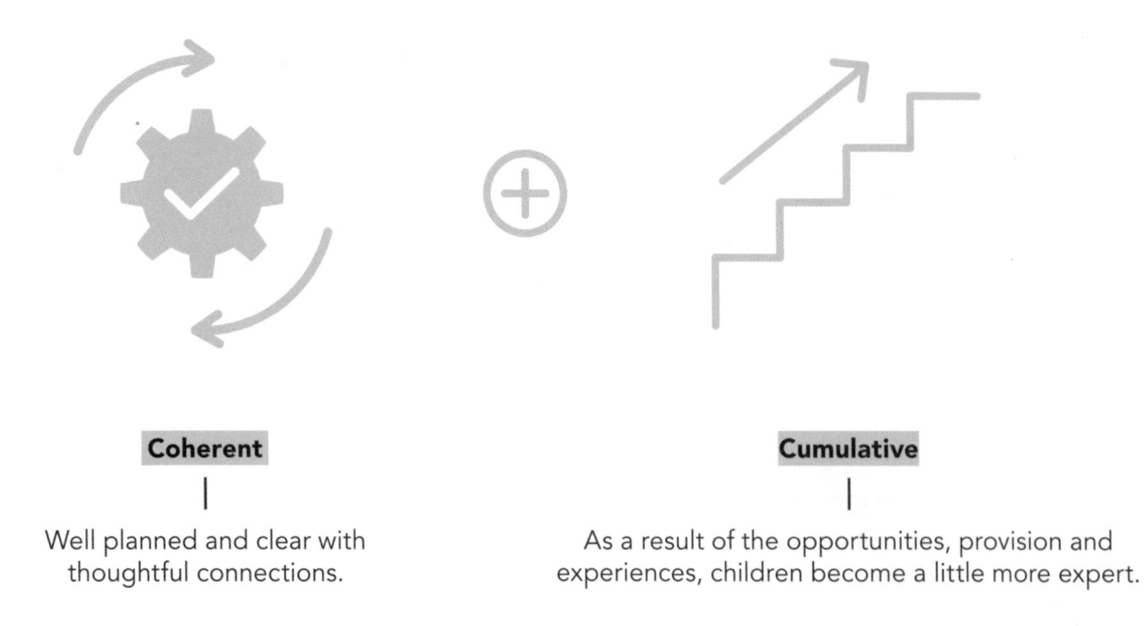

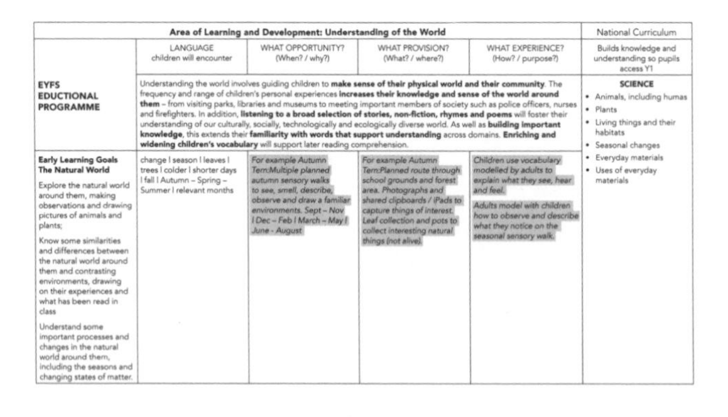

Area of Learning and Development: Understanding of the World					National Curriculum
	LANGUAGE children will encounter	WHAT OPPORTUNITY? (When? / why?)	WHAT PROVISION? (What? / where?)	WHAT EXPERIENCE? (How? / purpose?)	Builds knowledge and understanding so pupils access Y1
EYFS EDUCTIONAL PROGRAMME	Understanding the world involves guiding children to **make sense of their physical world and their community**. The frequency and range of children's personal experiences **increases their knowledge and sense of the world around them** – from visiting parks, libraries and museums to meeting important members of society such as police officers, nurses and firefighters. In addition, **listening to a broad selection of stories, non-fiction, rhymes and poems** will foster their understanding of our culturally, socially, technologically and ecologically diverse world. As well as **building important knowledge**, this extends their **familiarity with words that support understanding** across domains. **Enriching and widening children's vocabulary** will support later reading comprehension.				**SCIENCE** • Animals, including humas • Plants • Living things and their habitats • Seasonal changes • Everyday materials • Uses of everyday materials
Early Learning Goals The Natural World Explore the natural world around them, making observations and drawing pictures of animals and plants; Know some similarities and differences between the natural world around them and contrasting environments, drawing on their experiences and what has been read in class Understand some important processes and changes in the natural world around them, including the seasons and changing states of matter.	change I season I leaves I trees I colder I shorter days I fall I Autumn – Spring – Summer I relevant months	*For example Autumn Tem:Multiple planned autumn sensory walks to see, smell, describe, observe and draw a familiar environments. Sept – Nov I Dec – Feb I March – May I June - August*	*For example Autumn Tem:Planned route through school grounds and forest area. Photographs and shared clipboards / iPads to capture things of interest. Leaf collection and pots to collect interesting natural things (not alive).*	*Children use vocabulary modelled by adults to explain what they see, hear and feel.* *Adults model with children how to observe and describe what they notice on the seasonal sensory walk.*	

Coherent

Well planned and clear with thoughtful connections.

Cumulative

As a result of the opportunities, provision and experiences, children become a little more expert.

Granular

Visible explanations showcase a few examples of how the EYFS operates

Early learning goals (ELGs) are end-of-year outcomes – they are not a curriculum. They exist to prompt thought and discussion about how well pupils are securing the knowledge they need for a good level of development and KS1 readiness.

Communication and language → Spoken language

<table>
<tr><th colspan="5">Area of learning and development: Communication and language</th><th>National curriculum</th></tr>
<tr><td rowspan="2">EYFS EDUCATIONAL PROGRAMME
(DfE, 2023)</td><td>LANGUAGE
children will encounter</td><td>WHAT OPPORTUNITY?
(When? Why?)</td><td>WHAT PROVISION?
(What? Where?)</td><td>WHAT EXPERIENCE?
(How? Purpose?)</td><td rowspan="3">Spoken language, Years 1-6 (DfE, 2013)
'Pupils should be taught to:
• Listen and respond appropriately to adults and their peers.
• Ask relevant questions to extend their understanding and knowledge.
• Use relevant strategies to build their vocabulary.
• Articulate and justify answers, arguments and opinions.
• Give well-structured descriptions, explanations and narratives for different purposes, including for expressing feelings.
• Maintain attention and participate actively in collaborative conversations, staying on topic and initiating and responding to comments.
• Use spoken language to develop understanding through speculating, hypothesising, imagining and exploring ideas.
• Speak audibly and fluently with an increasing command of Standard English.
• Participate in discussions, presentations, performances, role play, improvisations and debates.
• Gain, maintain and monitor the interest of the listener(s).
• Consider and evaluate different viewpoints, attending to and building on the contributions of others.
• Select and use appropriate registers for effective communication.'</td></tr>
<tr><td colspan="4">'The development of children's spoken language underpins all seven areas of learning and development. Children's back-and-forth interactions from an early age form the foundations for language and cognitive development. The number and quality of the conversations they have with adults and peers throughout the day in a language-rich environment is crucial. By commenting on what children are interested in or doing, and echoing back what they say with new vocabulary added, practitioners will build children's language effectively. Reading frequently to children, and engaging them actively in stories, non-fiction, rhymes and poems, and then providing them with extensive opportunities to use and embed new words in a range of contexts, will give children the opportunity to thrive. Through conversation, story-telling and role play, where children share their ideas with support and modelling from their teacher, and sensitive questioning that invites them to elaborate, children become comfortable using a rich range of vocabulary and language structures.'</td></tr>
<tr><td>ELG: Listening, attention and understanding
'Children at the expected level of development will:
• Listen attentively and respond to what they hear with relevant questions, comments and actions when being read to and during whole class discussions and small group interactions.
• Make comments about what they have heard and ask questions to clarify their understanding.
• Hold conversation when engaged in back-and-forth exchanges with their teacher and peers.'
ELG: Speaking
'Children at the expected level of development will:
• Participate in small group, class and one-to-one discussions, offering their own ideas, using recently introduced vocabulary.
• Offer explanations for why things might happen, making use of recently introduced vocabulary from stories, non-fiction, rhymes and poems when appropriate.
• Express their ideas and feelings about their experiences using full sentences, including use of past, present and future tenses and making use of conjunctions, with modelling and support from their teacher.'</td><td></td><td></td><td></td><td></td></tr>
</table>

Early learning goals are end-of-year outcomes – they are not a curriculum. They exist to prompt thought and discussion about how well pupils are securing the knowledge they need for a good level of development and KS1 readiness.

Physical development → PSHE and PE

	Area of learning and development: Physical development				National curriculum
EYFS EDUCATIONAL PROGRAMME (DfE, 2023)	LANGUAGE children will encounter	WHAT OPPORTUNITY? (When? Why?)	WHAT PROVISION? (What? Where?)	WHAT EXPERIENCE? (How? Purpose?)	**The school curriculum in England (DfE, 2013)** 'Every state-funded school must offer a curriculum which is balanced and broadly based and which: • Promotes the spiritual, moral, cultural, mental and physical development of pupils at the school and of society. • Prepares pupils at the school for the opportunities, responsibilities and experiences of later life.' **Health and wellbeing (PSHE Association, 2020)** 'Pupils learn: • About what keeping healthy means; different ways to keep healthy. • About how physical activity helps us to stay healthy; and ways to be physically active everyday. • About why sleep is important and different ways to rest and relax. • About different ways to learn and play; recognising the importance of knowing when to take a break from time online or TV. • About the people who help us to stay physically healthy.'
	'**Physical activity is vital** in children's all-round development, enabling them to pursue **happy, healthy and active lives**. Gross and fine motor experiences develop incrementally throughout early childhood, starting with **sensory explorations** and the development of a child's **strength, co-ordination and positional** awareness through tummy time, crawling and play movement with both objects and adults. By creating **games and providing opportunities for play** both indoors and outdoors, adults can support children to develop their **core strength, stability, balance, spatial awareness, co-ordination and agility**. Gross motor skills provide the foundation for developing healthy bodies and social and emotional well-being. Fine motor control and precision helps with hand-eye co-ordination, which is later linked to early literacy. **Repeated and varied opportunities to explore and play** with small world activities, puzzles, arts and crafts and the practice of using small tools, with feedback and support from adults, allow children to develop **proficiency, control and confidence**.'				
ELG: Gross motor skills 'Children at the expected level of development will: • Negotiate space and obstacles safely, with consideration for themselves and others. • Demonstrate strength, balance and coordination when playing. • Move energetically, such as running, jumping, dancing, hopping, skipping and climbing.' **ELG: Fine motor skills** 'Children at the expected level of development will: • Hold a pencil effectively in preparation for fluent writing – using the tripod grip in almost all cases. • Use a range of small tools, including scissors, paint brushes and cutlery. • Begin to show accuracy and care when drawing.'					

Early learning goals are end-of-year outcomes – they are not a curriculum. They exist to prompt thought and discussion about how well pupils are securing the knowledge they need for a good level of development and KS1 readiness.

Personal, social and emotional development → PSHE

<table>
<tr><th colspan="5">Area of learning and development: Personal, social and emotional development</th><th>National curriculum</th></tr>
<tr><td rowspan="2">EYFS EDUCATIONAL PROGRAMME
(DfE, 2023)</td><td>LANGUAGE
children will encounter</td><td>WHAT OPPORTUNITY?
(When? Why?)</td><td>WHAT PROVISION?
(What? Where?)</td><td>WHAT EXPERIENCE?
(How? Purpose?)</td><td rowspan="3">Health and wellbeing (PSHE Association, 2020)
'Pupils learn:
• About what keeping healthy means; different ways to keep healthy.
• About how physical activity helps us to stay healthy; and ways to be physically active everyday.
• About why sleep is important and different ways to rest and relax.
• Simple hygiene routines that can stop germs from spreading.
• How to keep safe in the sun and protect skin from sun damage.
• About different ways to learn and play; recognising the importance of knowing when to take a break from time online or TV.
• About different feelings that humans can experience.
• How to recognise and name different feelings.
• How feelings can affect people's bodies and how they behave.
• How to recognise what others might be feeling.
• To recognise that not everyone feels the same at the same time, or feels the same about the same things.
• About ways of sharing feelings; a range of words to describe feelings.
• About things that help people feel good.
• Different things they can do to manage big feelings, to help calm themselves down and/or change their mood when they don't feel good.
• To recognise when they need help with feelings; that it is important to ask for help with feelings; and how to ask for it.
• About change and loss (including death); to identify feelings associated with this; to recognise what helps people to feel better.'</td></tr>
<tr><td colspan="4">'Children's personal, social and emotional development (PSED) is crucial for children to lead healthy and happy lives, and is fundamental to their cognitive development. Underpinning their personal development are the important attachments that shape their social world. Strong, warm and supportive relationships with adults enable children to learn how to understand their own feelings and those of others. Children should be supported to manage emotions, develop a positive sense of self, set themselves simple goals, have confidence in their own abilities, to persist and wait for what they want and direct attention as necessary. Through adult modelling and guidance, they will learn how to look after their bodies, including healthy eating, and manage personal needs independently. Through supported interaction with other children, they learn how to make good friendships, co-operate and resolve conflicts peaceably. These attributes will provide a secure platform from which children can achieve at school and in later life.'</td></tr>
<tr><td>ELG: Self-regulation
'Children at the expected level of development will:
• Show an understanding of their own feelings and those of others, and begin to regulate their behaviour accordingly.
• Set and work towards simple goals, being able to wait for what they want and control their immediate impulses when appropriate.
• Give focused attention to what the teacher says, responding appropriately even when engaged in activity, and show an ability to follow instructions involving several ideas or actions.'
ELG: Managing self
'Children at the expected level of development will:
• Be confident to try new activities and show independence, resilience and perseverance in the face of challenge.
• Explain the reasons for rules, know right from wrong and try to behave accordingly.
• Manage their own basic hygiene and personal needs, including dressing, going to the toilet and understanding the importance of healthy food choices.'
ELG: Building relationships
'Children at the expected level of development will:
• Work and play cooperatively and take turns with others.
• Form positive attachments to adults and friendships with peers.
• Show sensitivity to their own and to others' needs.'</td><td></td><td></td><td></td><td></td></tr>
</table>

Early learning goals are end-of-year outcomes – they are not a curriculum. They exist to prompt thought and discussion about how well pupils are securing the knowledge they need for a good level of development and KS1 readiness.

Literacy → Reading and writing

<table>
<tr><th colspan="5">Area of learning and development: Literacy</th><th>National curriculum</th></tr>
<tr><td rowspan="2">EYFS EDUCATIONAL PROGRAMME
(DfE, 2023)</td><td>LANGUAGE
children will encounter</td><td>WHAT OPPORTUNITY?
(When? Why?)</td><td>WHAT PROVISION?
(What? Where?)</td><td>WHAT EXPERIENCE?
(How? Purpose?)</td><td rowspan="3">Year 1 word reading (DfE, 2013)
'Pupils should be taught to:
• Apply phonic knowledge and skills as the route to decode words.
• Respond speedily with the correct sound to graphemes (letters or groups of letters) for all 40+ phonemes, including, where applicable, alternative sounds for graphemes.
• Read accurately by blending sounds in unfamiliar words containing GPCs that have been taught.
• Read common exception words, noting unusual correspondences between spelling and sound and where these occur in the word.
• Read words containing taught GPCs and –s, –es, –ing, –ed, –er and –est endings.
• Read other words of more than one syllable that contain taught GPCs.
• Read words with contractions (for example, I'm, I'll, we'll), and understand that the apostrophe represents the omitted letter(s).
• Read aloud accurately books that are consistent with their developing phonic knowledge and that do not require them to use other strategies to work out words.
• Re-read these books to build up their fluency and confidence in word reading.'</td></tr>
<tr><td colspan="4">'It is crucial for children to develop a life-long love of reading. Reading consists of two dimensions: language comprehension and word reading. Language comprehension (necessary for both reading and writing) starts from birth. It only develops when adults talk with children about the world around them and the books (stories and non-fiction) they read with them, and enjoy rhymes, poems and songs together. Skilled word reading, taught later, involves both the speedy working out of the pronunciation of unfamiliar printed words (decoding) and the speedy recognition of familiar printed words. Writing involves transcription (spelling and handwriting) and composition (articulating ideas and structuring them in speech, before writing).'</td></tr>
<tr><td>ELG: Comprehension
'Children at the expected level of development will:
• Demonstrate understanding of what has been read to them by retelling stories and narratives using their own words and recently introduced vocabulary.
• Anticipate – where appropriate – key events in stories.
• Use and understand recently introduced vocabulary during discussions about stories, non-fiction, rhymes and poems and during role-play.'
ELG: Word reading
'Children at the expected level of development will:
• Say a sound for each letter in the alphabet and at least 10 digraphs.
• Read words consistent with their phonic knowledge by sound-blending.
• Read aloud simple sentences and books that are consistent with their phonic knowledge, including some common exception words.'
ELG: Writing
'Children at the expected level of development will:
• Write recognisable letters, most of which are correctly formed.
• Spell words by identifying sounds in them and representing the sounds with a letter or letters.
• Write simple phrases and sentences that can be read by others.'</td><td></td><td></td><td></td><td></td></tr>
</table>

Early learning goals are end-of-year outcomes – they are not a curriculum. They exist to prompt thought and discussion about how well pupils are securing the knowledge they need for a good level of development and KS1 readiness.

Mathematics → Mathematics

<table>
<tr><th colspan="5">Area of learning and development: Mathematics</th><th>National curriculum</th></tr>
<tr><td rowspan="2">EYFS EDUCATIONAL PROGRAMME
(DfE, 2023)</td><td>LANGUAGE
children will encounter</td><td>WHAT OPPORTUNITY?
(When? Why?)</td><td>WHAT PROVISION?
(What? Where?)</td><td>WHAT EXPERIENCE?
(How? Purpose?)</td><td rowspan="3">Year 1 number and place value (DfE, 2013)
'Pupils should be taught to:
• Count to and across 100, forwards and backwards, beginning with 0 or 1, or from any given number.
• Count, read and write numbers to 100 in numerals; count in multiples of twos, fives and tens.
• Given a number, identify one more and one less.
• Identify and represent numbers using objects and pictorial representations including the number line, and use the language of: equal to, more than, less than (fewer), most, least.
• Read and write numbers from 1 to 20 in numerals and words.'</td></tr>
<tr><td colspan="4">'Developing a strong grounding in number is essential so that all children develop the necessary building blocks to excel mathematically. Children should be able to count confidently, develop a deep understanding of the numbers to 10, the relationships between them and the patterns within those numbers. By providing frequent and varied opportunities to build and apply this understanding - such as using manipulatives, including small pebbles and tens frames for organising counting - children will develop a secure base of knowledge and vocabulary from which mastery of mathematics is built. In addition, it is important that the curriculum includes rich opportunities for children to develop their spatial reasoning skills across all areas of mathematics including shape, space and measures. It is important that children develop positive attitudes and interests in mathematics, look for patterns and relationships, spot connections, 'have a go', talk to adults and peers about what they notice and not be afraid to make mistakes.'</td></tr>
<tr><td>ELG: Number
'Children at the expected level of development will:
• Have a deep understanding of number to 10, including the composition of each number.
• Subitise (recognise quantities without counting) up to 5.
• Automatically recall (without reference to rhymes, counting or other aids) number bonds up to 5 (including subtraction facts) and some number bonds to 10, including double facts.'
ELG: Numerical patterns
'Children at the expected level of development will:
• Verbally count beyond 20, recognising the pattern of the counting system.
• Compare quantities up to 10 in different contexts, recognising when one quantity is greater than, less than or the same as the other quantity.
• Explore and represent patterns within numbers up to 10, including evens and odds, double facts and how quantities can be distributed equally.'</td><td></td><td></td><td></td><td></td></tr>
</table>

Early learning goals are end-of-year outcomes – they are not a curriculum. They exist to prompt thought and discussion about how well pupils are securing the knowledge they need for a good level of development and KS1 readiness.

Understanding the world → Science

	Area of learning and development: Understanding the world				National curriculum
EYFS EDUCATIONAL PROGRAMME (DfE, 2023)	LANGUAGE children will encounter	WHAT OPPORTUNITY? (When? Why?)	WHAT PROVISION? (What? Where?)	WHAT EXPERIENCE? (How? Purpose?)	Builds knowledge and understanding so pupils can access Year 1
	'Understanding the world involves guiding children to make sense of their physical world and their community. The frequency and range of children's personal experiences increases their knowledge and sense of the world around them – from visiting parks, libraries and museums to meeting important members of society such as police officers, nurses and firefighters. In addition, **listening to a broad selection of stories, non-fiction, rhymes and poems** will foster their understanding of our culturally, socially, technologically and ecologically diverse world. As well as **building important knowledge**, this extends their **familiarity with words that support understanding** across domains. **Enriching and widening children's vocabulary** will support later reading comprehension.'				**SCIENCE** • Animals, including humans. • Plants. • Living things and their habitats. • Seasonal changes. • Everyday materials. • Uses of everyday materials.
ELG: The natural world 'Children at the expected level of development will: • Explore the natural world around them, making observations and drawing pictures of animals and plants. • Know some similarities and differences between the natural world around them and contrasting environments, drawing on their experiences and what has been read in class. • Understand some important processes and changes in the natural world around them.'	*For example, change / season / leaves / trees / colder / shorter days / fall / autumn – winter – spring – summer / relevant months*	*For example, autumn term: multiple planned autumn sensory walks to see, smell, describe, observe and draw familiar environments. Sept-Nov / Dec-Feb / March-May / June-August*	*For example, autumn term: planned route through school grounds and forest area. Photographs and shared clipboards/iPads to capture things of interest. Leaf collection and pots to collect interesting natural things (not alive).*	*For example, children use vocabulary modelled by adults to explain what they see, hear and feel. Adults model with children how to observe and describe what they notice on the seasonal sensory walk.*	

Early learning goals are end-of-year outcomes – they are not a curriculum. They exist to prompt thought and discussion about how well pupils are securing the knowledge they need for a good level of development and KS1 readiness.

People, culture and communities → Geography

	Area of learning and development: Understanding the world				National curriculum
EYFS EDUCATIONAL PROGRAMME (DfE, 2023)	LANGUAGE children will encounter	WHAT OPPORTUNITY? (When? Why?)	WHAT PROVISION? (What? Where?)	WHAT EXPERIENCE? (How? Purpose?)	Builds knowledge and understanding so pupils can access Year 1
	'Understanding the world involves guiding children to make sense of their physical world and their community. The frequency and range of children's personal experiences increases their knowledge and sense of the world around them – from visiting parks, libraries and museums to meeting important members of society such as police officers, nurses and firefighters. In addition, **listening to a broad selection of stories, non-fiction, rhymes and poems** will foster their understanding of our culturally, socially, technologically and ecologically diverse world. As well as **building important knowledge**, this extends their **familiarity with words that support understanding** across domains. **Enriching and widening children's vocabulary** will support later reading comprehension.'				**KS1 geography (DfE, 2013)** • 'Locational knowledge: name and locate the world's seven continents and five oceans; name, locate and identify characteristics of the four countries and capital cities of the United Kingdom and its surrounding seas. • Place knowledge: understand geographical similarities and differences of a small area of the United Kingdom, and of a small area in a contrasting non-European country. • Human and physical geography: identify seasonal and daily weather patterns in the United Kingdom and the location of hot and cold areas of the world in relation to the Equator and the North and South Poles; use basic geographical vocabulary. • Geographical skills and fieldwork: use world maps, atlases and globes to identify the United Kingdom and its countries; use simple compass directions (North, South, East and West); use simple fieldwork and observational skills to study the geography of their school and its grounds.'
ELG: People, culture and communities 'Children at the expected level of development will: • Describe their immediate environment using knowledge from observation, discussion, stories, non-fiction texts and maps. • Know some similarities and differences between different religious and cultural communities in this country, drawing on their experiences and what has been read in class. • Explain some similarities and differences between life in this country and life in other countries.'					

Early learning goals are end-of-year outcomes – they are not a curriculum. They exist to prompt thought and discussion about how well pupils are securing the knowledge they need for a good level of development and KS1 readiness.

Past and present → History

Area of learning and development: Understanding the world					National curriculum
	LANGUAGE children will encounter	WHAT OPPORTUNITY? (When? Why?)	WHAT PROVISION? (What? Where?)	WHAT EXPERIENCE? (How? Purpose?)	Builds knowledge and understanding so pupils can access Year 1
EYFS EDUCATIONAL PROGRAMME (DfE, 2023)	'Understanding the world involves guiding children to make sense of their physical world and their community. The frequency and range of children's personal experiences increases their knowledge and sense of the world around them – from visiting parks, libraries and museums to meeting important members of society such as police officers, nurses and firefighters. In addition, **listening to a broad selection of stories, non-fiction, rhymes and poems** will foster their understanding of our culturally, socially, technologically and ecologically diverse world. As well as **building important knowledge**, this extends their **familiarity with words that support understanding** across domains. **Enriching and widening children's vocabulary** will support later reading comprehension.'				**HISTORY** • Changes within living memory. • Changes beyond living memory. • Significant individuals. • Significant historical events, festivals or celebrations.
ELG: Past and present 'Children at the expected level of development will: • - Talk about the lives of the people around them and their roles in society. • Know some similarities and differences between things in the past and now, drawing on their experiences and what has been read in class. • Understand the past through settings, characters and events encountered in books read in class and storytelling.'					

Early learning goals are end-of-year outcomes – they are not a curriculum. They exist to prompt thought and discussion about how well pupils are securing the knowledge they need for a good level of development and KS1 readiness.

Expressive arts and design → Design and technology

<table>
<tr><th colspan="5">Area of learning and development: Expressive arts and design</th><th>National curriculum</th></tr>
<tr><td rowspan="2">EYFS EDUCATIONAL PROGRAMME
(DfE, 2023)</td><td>LANGUAGE
children will encounter</td><td>WHAT OPPORTUNITY?
(When? Why?)</td><td>WHAT PROVISION?
(What? Where?)</td><td>WHAT EXPERIENCE?
(How? Purpose?)</td><td>Builds knowledge and understanding so pupils can access Year 1</td></tr>
<tr><td colspan="4">'The development of children's artistic and cultural awareness supports their imagination and creativity. It is important that children have regular opportunities to engage with the arts, enabling them to explore and play with a wide range of media and materials. The quality and variety of what children see, hear and participate in is crucial for developing their understanding, self-expression, vocabulary and ability to communicate through the arts. The frequency, repetition and depth of their experiences are fundamental to their progress in interpreting and appreciating what they hear, respond to and observe.'</td><td rowspan="2">KS1 design and technology (DfE, 2013)
'When designing and making, pupils should be taught to:
• Design purposeful, functional, appealing products for themselves and other users based on design criteria.
• Generate, develop, model and communicate their ideas through talking, drawing, templates, mock-ups and, where appropriate, information and communication technology.
• Select from and use a range of tools and equipment to perform practical tasks [for example, cutting, shaping, joining and finishing].
• Select from and use a wide range of materials and components, including construction materials, textiles and ingredients, according to their characteristics.
• Explore and evaluate a range of existing products.
• Evaluate their ideas and products against design criteria.
• Build structures, exploring how they can be made stronger, stiffer and more stable.
• Explore and use mechanisms [for example, levers, sliders, wheels and axles], in their products.'</td></tr>
<tr><td>ELG: Creating with materials
'Children at the expected level of development will:
• Safely use and explore a variety of materials, tools and techniques, experimenting with colour, design, texture, form and function.
• Share their creations, explaining the process they have used.
Make use of props and materials when role playing characters in narratives and stories.'</td><td></td><td></td><td></td><td></td></tr>
</table>

Early learning goals are end-of-year outcomes – they are not a curriculum. They exist to prompt thought and discussion about how well pupils are securing the knowledge they need for a good level of development and KS1 readiness.

People, culture and communities → Religious education

	Area of learning and development: Understanding the world				National curriculum
	LANGUAGE children will encounter	WHAT OPPORTUNITY? (When? Why?)	WHAT PROVISION? (What? Where?)	WHAT EXPERIENCE? (How? Purpose?)	Builds knowledge and understanding so pupils can access Year 1
EYFS EDUCATIONAL PROGRAMME (DfE, 2023)	'Understanding the world involves guiding children to make sense of their physical world and their community. The frequency and range of children's personal experiences increases their knowledge and sense of the world around them – from visiting parks, libraries and museums to meeting important members of society such as police officers, nurses and firefighters. In addition, **listening to a broad selection of stories, non-fiction, rhymes and poems** will foster their understanding of our culturally, socially, technologically and ecologically diverse world. As well as **building important knowledge**, this extends their **familiarity with words that support understanding** across domains. **Enriching and widening children's vocabulary** will support later reading comprehension.'				**Does God want Christians to look after the world?** (Christianity) **What gift might Christians in my town have given Jesus if he had been born here rather than in Bethlehem?** (Christianity) **Was it always easy for Jesus to show friendship?** (Christianity) **Why was Jesus welcomed like a king or celebrity on Palm Sunday?** (Christianity) **Is Shabbat important to Jewish children?** (Judaism) **Are Rosh Hashanah and Yom Kippur important to Jewish children?** (Judaism)
ELG: People, culture and communities 'Children at the expected level of development will: • Describe their immediate environment using knowledge from observation, discussion, stories, non-fiction texts and maps. • Know some similarities and differences between different religious and cultural communities in this country, drawing on their experiences and what has been read in class. • Explain some similarities and differences between life in this country and life in other countries.'		**What makes people special?** (Christianity, Judaism) **What is Christmas?** (Christianity) **How do people celebrate?** (Islam/Judaism) **What is Easter?** (Christianity) **What can we learn from stories?** (Christianity, Islam, Hinduism, Sikhism) **What makes people special?** (Christianity, Islam, Judaism)			

The content is an example from Discovery RE

Early learning goals are end-of-year outcomes – they are not a curriculum. They exist to prompt thought and discussion about how well pupils are securing the knowledge they need for a good level of development and KS1 readiness.

Expressive arts and design → Art and design

<table>
<tr><td colspan="5">Area of learning and development: Expressive arts and design</td><td>National curriculum</td></tr>
<tr><td rowspan="2">EYFS EDUCATIONAL PROGRAMME
(DfE, 2023)</td><td>LANGUAGE
children will encounter</td><td>WHAT OPPORTUNITY?
(When? Why?)</td><td>WHAT PROVISION?
(What? Where?)</td><td>WHAT EXPERIENCE?
(How? Purpose?)</td><td>Builds knowledge and understanding so pupils can access Year 1</td></tr>
<tr><td colspan="4">'The development of children's artistic and cultural awareness supports their imagination and creativity. It is important that children have regular opportunities to engage with the arts, enabling them to explore and play with a wide range of media and materials. The quality and variety of what children see, hear and participate in is crucial for developing their understanding, self-expression, vocabulary and ability to communicate through the arts. The frequency, repetition and depth of their experiences are fundamental to their progress in interpreting and appreciating what they hear, respond to and observe.'</td><td rowspan="2">KS1 art and design (DfE, 2013)
'Pupils should be taught:
• To use a range of materials creatively to design and make products.
• To use drawing, painting and sculpture to develop and share their ideas, experiences and imagination.
• To develop a wide range of art and design techniques in using colour, pattern, texture, line, shape, form and space.
• About the work of a range of artists, craft makers and designers, describing the differences and similarities between different practices and disciplines, and making links to their own work.'</td></tr>
<tr><td>ELG: Creating with materials
'Children at the expected level of development will:
• Safely use and explore a variety of materials, tools and techniques, experimenting with colour, design, texture, form and function.
• Share their creations, explaining the process they have used.
• Make use of props and materials when role playing characters in narratives and stories.'</td><td></td><td></td><td></td><td></td></tr>
</table>

Early learning goals are end-of-year outcomes – they are not a curriculum. They exist to prompt thought and discussion about how well pupils are securing the knowledge they need for a good level of development and KS1 readiness.

Expressive arts and design → Music

	Area of learning and development: Expressive arts and design				National curriculum
	LANGUAGE children will encounter	WHAT OPPORTUNITY? (When? Why?)	WHAT PROVISION? (What? Where?)	WHAT EXPERIENCE? (How? Purpose?)	Builds knowledge and understanding so pupils can access Year 1
EYFS EDUCATIONAL PROGRAMME (DfE, 2023)	'The development of children's **artistic and cultural awareness** supports their **imagination and creativity**. It is important that children have regular opportunities to engage with the arts, enabling them to explore and play with a wide range of media and materials. The quality and variety of what children see, hear and participate in is crucial for **developing their understanding, self-expression, vocabulary and ability to communicate** through the arts. The frequency, repetition and depth of their experiences are fundamental to their progress in interpreting and appreciating what they hear, respond to and observe.'				**KS1 music (DfE, 2013)** 'Pupils should be taught to: • Use their voices expressively and creatively by singing songs and speaking chants and rhymes. • Play tuned and untuned instruments musically. • Listen with concentration and understanding to a range of high-quality live and recorded music. • Experiment with, create, select and combine sounds using the inter-related dimensions of music.'
ELG: Being imaginative and expressive 'Children at the expected level of development will: • Invent, adapt and recount narratives and stories with peers and their teacher. • Sing a range of well-known nursery rhymes and songs. • Perform songs, rhymes, poems and stories with others, and – when appropriate – try to move in time with music.'					

Early learning goals are end-of-year outcomes – they are not a curriculum. They exist to prompt thought and discussion about how well pupils are securing the knowledge they need for a good level of development and KS1 readiness.

Ask yourself...

If you were asked these questions, how would you answer?

1. How do you know your provision is planned strategically as well as responding to the child at the point of provision?

2. What is the impact of the curriculum you offer? How do you know?

3. How do you know the intended learning is transferring to children's long-term memory?

4. What changes to provision are needed to ensure children's learning experiences are generative?

5. How effectively do your teaching and provision contribute to learning?

6. How well does the provision develop the foundational knowledge that pupils need in order to access the next stage of their education?

Bibliography

A list of publications that have been referenced or have inspired this book

Alexander, R. (2008) *Towards Dialogic Teaching: rethinking classroom talk* (fourth edition), Dialogos UK

Coe, R., Rauch, C.J., Kime, S. & Singleton, D. (2020) *Great Teaching Toolkit: evidence review*, Evidence Based Education, www.greatteaching.com

Crystal, D. (2006) *How Language Works*, Penguin Books

Department for Education. (2013) *The National Curriculum in England Key stages 1 and 2 framework document*, https://assets.publishing.service.gov.uk/government/uploads/system/uploads/attachment_data/file/425601/PRIMARY_national_curriculum.pdf

Department for Education. (2019) *Relationships Education, Relationships and Sex Education (RSE) and Health Education: statutory guidance for governing bodies, proprietors, head teachers, principals, senior leadership teams, teachers*, https://assets.publishing.service.gov.uk/government/uploads/system/uploads/attachment_data/file/1090195/Relationships_Education_RSE_and_Health_Education.pdf

Department for Education. (2021) *Development Matters: non-statutory curriculum guidance for the early years foundation stage*, https://assets.publishing.service.gov.uk/government/uploads/system/uploads/attachment_data/file/1007446/6.7534_DfE_Development_Matters_Report_and_illustrations_web__2_.pdf

Department for Education. (2023) *Statutory Framework for the Early Years Foundation Stage*, https://assets.publishing.service.gov.uk/government/uploads/system/uploads/attachment_data/file/1168794/EYFS_framework_From_September_2023.pdf

Early Education. (2021) *Birth to 5 Matters: non-statutory guidance for the early years foundation stage*, https://birthto5matters.org.uk/wp-content/uploads/2021/03/Birthto5Matters-download.pdf

Ebbinghaus, H. (1885/1913) *Memory: a contribution to experimental psychology*, Teachers College, Columbia University

Education Endowment Foundation. (2017) *Dialogic Teaching: evaluation report and executive summary*, bit.ly/43nbOQB

Education Endowment Foundation. (2022) *High Quality Interactions in the Early Years: the 'ShREC' approach*, bit.ly/3rruK3e

Featherstone, S. (2017) *Making Sense of Neuroscience in the Early Years*, Bloomsbury

Fiorella, L. & Mayer, R.E. (2016) 'Eight ways to promote generative learning', *Educational Psychology Review*, 28, pp.717-741

Goddard Blythe, S. (2017) *Attention, Balance and Coordination: the ABC of learning success* (second edition), Wiley Blackwell

Goddard Blythe, S. (2023) *Reflexes, Movement, Learning and Behaviour: analysing and unblocking neuro-motor immaturity*, Hawthorn Press

Kearns, T. & Lee, D. (2015) *General Psychology: an introduction*, NOBA Project

Law, J., Charlton, J., Dockrell, J., Gascoigne, M., McKean, C. & Theakston, A. (2017) *Early Language Development: needs, provision, and intervention for preschool children from socio- economically disadvantaged backgrounds*, Education Endowment Foundation, bit.ly/3NlhEq1

Mccrea, P. (2021) https://twitter.com/PepsMccrea/status/1534596124115447811

Mercer, N., Wegerif, R. & Dawes, L. (1999) 'Children's talk and the development of reasoning in the classroom', *British Educational Research Journal*, 25(1), pp.95-111

Nigg, J.T. (2017) *Getting Ahead of ADHD: what next-generation science says about treatments that work – and how you can make them work for your child*, Guilford Press

Oakhill, J., Cain, K. & Elbro, C. (2014) *Understanding and Teaching Reading Comprehension: a handbook*, Routledge

Osborne, R.J. & Wittrock, M.C. (1983) 'Learning science: a generative process', *Science Education*, 67(4), pp.489-508

PSHE Association. (2020) *Programme of Study for PSHE Education: key stages 1-5*, https://pshe-association.org.uk/guidance/ks1-5/planning/long-term-planning

Roediger, H.L. & Gallo, D.A. (2002) 'Levels of processing: some unanswered questions' in M. Naveh-Benjamin, M. Moscovitch & H.L. Roediger (eds.), *Perspectives on Human Memory and Cognitive Aging: essays in honour of Fergus Craik* (pp.28-47), Psychology Press

Rosenshine, B. (2012) 'Principles of instruction: research-based strategies that all teachers should know', *American Educator*, 36(1), pp.12-19

Schacter, D.L., Dobbins, I.G. & Schnyer, D.M. (2004) 'Specificity of priming: a cognitive neuroscience perspective', *Nature Reviews Neuroscience*, 5, pp.853-862

Shea, J. (2021) 'Cognitive science v neuroscience: retrieval at the start of a lesson or not?' (blog post), *Peer Reviewed Education Blog*, https://peerreviewededucationblog.com/2021/02/06/cognitive-science-v-neuroscience-retrieval-at-the-start-of-a-lesson-or-not

Sweller, J. (1994) 'Cognitive load theory, learning difficulty, and instructional design', *Learning and Instruction*, 4(4), pp.295-312

Tough, J. (1973) *Focus on Meaning: talking to some purpose with young children*, George Allen & Unwin

Tough, J. (1977a) *Talking and Learning: a guide to fostering communication skills in nursery and infant schools*, Ward Lock Educational/Drake Educational Associates

Tough, J. (1977b) *The Development of Meaning: a study of children's use of language*, George Allen & Unwin

von Tetzchner, S. (2023) *Typical and Atypical Child and Adolescent Development 4: cognition, intelligence and learning*, Routledge

Williams, M.S. & Shellenberger, S. (1996) *How Does Your Engine Run? A leader's guide to the ALERT program for self-regulation*, Therapy Works